The Standard & Poor's Guide
to Personal Finance

OTHER STANDARD & POOR'S BOOKS

THE STANDARD & POOR'S GUIDE
FOR THE NEW INVESTOR
by Nilus Mattive

THE STANDARD & POOR'S GUIDE
TO LONG-TERM INVESTING
by Joseph R. Tigue

THE STANDARD & POOR'S GUIDE
TO SAVING AND INVESTING FOR COLLEGE
by David J. Braverman

THE Standard & Poor's Guide to Personal Finance

TOM DOWNEY

McGRAW-HILL
New York | Chicago | San Francisco | Lisbon
London | Madrid | Mexico City | Milan | New Delhi
San Juan | Seoul | Singapore | Sydney | Toronto

The McGraw·Hill Companies

1 2 3 4 5 6 7 8 9 0 FGR/FGR 0 9 8 7 6 5

ISBN 0-07-144741-5

This publication is designed to provide accurate and authoritative information in regard to the subject matter covered. It is sold with the understanding that neither the author nor the publisher is engaged in rendering legal, accounting, or other professional service. If legal advice or other expert assistance is required, the services of a competent professional person should be sought.—*From a declaration of principles jointly adopted by a committee of the American Bar Association and a committee of publishers*

McGraw-Hill books are available at special discounts to use as premiums and sales promotions, or for use in corporate training programs. For more information, please write to the Director of Special Sales, Professional Publishing, McGraw-Hill, Two Penn Plaza, New York, NY 10121-2298. Or contact your local bookstore.

 This book is printed on recycled, acid-free paper containing a minimum of 50% recycled de-inked paper.

Library of Congress Cataloging-in-Publication Data

Downey, Tom, 1968-
    The Standard & Poor's guide to personal finance / by Tom Downey.
        p. cm.
    ISBN 0-07-144741-5 (pbk. : alk. paper)
    1. Finance, Personal. I. Title: Standard and Poor's guide to personal finance. II. Title:
Guide to personal finance. III. Standard and Poor's Corporation. IV. Title.
    HG179.D697 2005
    332.024–dc22
                                                                                            2004028201

To Stephanie—my wife, my love, my inspiration

Contents

Acknowledgments

I want to thank everyone who helped make this book possible, starting with my wife Stephanie. I couldn't have done it without her. Thanks again, Steph. I also want to thank everyone at McGraw-Hill in general and Standard & Poor's in particular who was involved with this project, including Jim Branscome, Kelli Christiansen (my esteemed editor), George Gulla, and Laura Libretti. I'd also like to thank my friends and colleagues at Standard & Poor's Financial Communications—especially Carol Goodwin (now a former colleague), Brian Johnson, Nabil Lebbos, Ehrick Wright, and Mike Zargaj. And I'd be remiss if I didn't thank Elayne Sheridan for initially suggesting many years ago that I should write a book like this. Many thanks, too, to my good friends Mike Barton and Greg White for their counsel. And finally, I'd like to offer special words of thanks to my parents, for their optimism, love, and support, and to my sons Otis and Luke, for making me smile every day and to reflect on what a lucky person I am.

The Standard & Poor's Guide
to Personal Finance

Introduction

When I was preparing to write *The Standard & Poor's Guide to Personal Finance*, I went out and bought a spiral-bound notebook, like those commonly used by high school and college students, to devote to the project.

Inside the front cover was an extra page with information that I didn't need—a five-year calendar, metric conversion tables, etc. As I was in the process of tearing out that page, I happened to notice that it also contained a brief message under the heading "Be Positive! Creating a positive attitude is the key to effective studying." A list followed. Point number one said, "Relax—but be alert. Don't try to study when you are hungry or sleepy." Number two said, "Concentrate—try to push all worries or unrelated thoughts out of your mind." And number three said, "Motivate—get involved in the subject. Learn how a subject relates to you and the things you're interested in—then you'll want to learn more about it."

It dawned on me that by replacing the concept of studying with the concept of managing your money, the "Be Positive!" credo suddenly reflected the type of take-charge philosophy and confident, upbeat tone I wanted to express in these pages—particularly point number three. (Go back and reread the previous paragraph with those edits in mind and you'll see what I mean.)

The fact is, there are plenty of otherwise intelligent, capable people who don't yet have the confidence, self-awareness, trust, or financial vocabulary necessary to identify their financial needs and ask for help. But that doesn't mean they need to spend the rest of their lives in financial darkness. As numerous surveys and studies over the years have illustrated, there is a direct connection between financial confidence and your ability to accomplish some of life's most important short- and long-term goals. However, so much of the educational financial material currently available to ordinary people either treats them like dummies or is so full of lingo and unfamiliar concepts that it confuses more than enlightens.

Therefore, it was my goal to write an easy-to-read, "plain English" book about personal financial management that would stand out from the crowd and prove to be a comprehensive, concise, and indispensable resource for just about anyone. With topics that can be read in a single sitting and referred to again and again, this book will provide the information and insights necessary to help you do a better job of identifying your needs, quantifying your goals, and taking action. Instead of intimidating, overwhelming, or confusing readers, I tried to create a basic financial primer for those who might be turned off by too much information or feel bewildered by jargon and shop talk. You'll learn—and feel confident about learning and doing more—by having the basic information about each topic presented in a succinct, understandable, and encouraging manner.

Each of the chapters contains several different discussions related to one general theme. In the bigger picture, though, these conversations all tie together and complement each other throughout the course of the book. Together, they should motivate you to make well-informed decisions that have the potential to improve your financial well-being now and many years down the road.

I once had a boss who said, "In life, you can either bounce the ball or you can be bounced by the ball." He wasn't talking about money, but he could have been. If you're in control of your money, then you're bouncing the ball. If you're not in control, then the ball is bouncing you—or worse yet, rolling right over you. It's not a feeling that inspires confidence.

With that in mind, this book will talk about how to better control your money today and, by extension, how to start laying the groundwork for a more financially secure future.

CHAPTER 1

It's Your Financial Life— Take It Seriously

This book exists to help you identify key priorities and answer important questions related to your personal finances, but it can't do all of the work for you. Because while the topics it covers all revolve around money, the real subject of this book is actually you and—by extension—the other people who dwell in your financial household.

Think of it this way: You and your neighbor can both agree on what a $100 bill looks like, right? If you each received a card in the mail with a $100 bill in it, you would both understand, almost instinctively, that this particular piece of paper represents 100 American dollars, and that you could take it to the bank and exchange it for two $50 bills, or ten $10 bills, etc. In fact, anyone over the age of six would probably have the same response after opening a card like that: "Great. Someone sent me $100!"

But would that $100 bill also trigger identical emotions and spending decisions for you and your neighbor? Maybe not—because you aren't identical people, and you probably don't have identical financial priorities and instincts. Think about it. One of you might put the money in the bank; the other might spend it right away. Money isn't just a medium for exchange that allows us to make purchases. It's also a force that has the potential to reveal our innermost personality traits, our attitudes about life, and our dedication to pursuing life-changing goals for ourselves and the people we care about.

For some people, of course, money probably doesn't come with all that emotional baggage. But for almost everyone else, our relationship with money helps define who we are—and what we can achieve—in the world. Money, or a lack thereof, can represent and bring to mind social status ... opportunity ... security ... insecurity ... anxiety ... hope ... accomplishment ... greed ... generosity ... stress... peace of mind. You get the picture.

Whether you're rich or poor, young or old, a saver or a spender, or somewhere in between, money can be pretty overwhelming. One question usually leads to another, and quite often one potential solution opens the door to a whole new set of questions and options. What are your goals in life? How should you pursue them? What type of accounts should you use? What are the tax implications? What should you be doing now in order to continue supporting loved ones (or a business or charity) after you're gone? Why, and how, should you get the entire household involved in laying the groundwork for long-term financial security and confidence?

If you're still reading, then it's a safe bet that at least some of these questions and considerations probably hit close to home.

In an ideal world, of course, we would all recognize what a powerful force money can be in our lives, and we would all spend as much time as necessary learning more about money and taking care of good, old-fashioned financial planning—budgeting, saving, investing, etc. Well, guess what? It's not an ideal world, and many of us aren't so financially inclined.

The point is, this book is full of explanations and insights that will help you enhance the role of money in your life. But it's your own capacity for honest self-assessment and self-improvement that will actually transform these words on paper into a better future for everyone in your financial household. This book will teach you the basics about money and personal financial management, but a book alone is incapable of transforming your financial life. That's your job. As you work your way through each chapter, pause from time to time to ask yourself two important questions: What is your vision of the future? And what do you intend to do with—and about—this thing in your life called money?

It Takes All Hands to Get a Grip on Household Finances

Congratulations. Simply by reading the first few pages you've begun to contemplate (or recontemplate) the role of money in your life. Now it's time to take the next logical step and start thinking about the relationships the other people in your household have with money.

Why? Because unless each person in your household is 100 percent financially secure and self-reliant, the only way you'll all maximize your money is by working together as a team.

For example, it makes sense for the adults and teenagers in your home to sit down together in order to identify the individual financial goals of each person, as well as the shared goals of the entire household. The list you create together should be all-encompassing, but not trivial—jot down any significant long- and short-term objectives, and try to estimate the cost for each. Of course, if Junior casually mentions that he expects to buy an expensive new car immediately after getting his driver's license, this can also be the perfect occasion for you to put the brakes on that kind of wishful thinking.

If necessary, explain that as the head of the household you have the right and the responsibility to see that money is being managed efficiently all around, and that you expect the others to share in that responsibility. And remember that it's possible to do all of this without totally surrendering your own privacy. In other words, feel free to discuss specific financial goals with your kids, but don't necessarily feel obliged to reveal intimate details about your net worth and life savings. (Parents must decide for themselves how much information sharing is too much.)

Now please allow a brief aside. It might not even seem relevant at first, but it is.

In the military, people have a tendency to talk about two kinds of objectives: strategic and tactical. As the words imply, one is related to strategy (the big picture) and one is related to tactics (the movement of planes in the air, ships at sea, soldiers on the ground, and so on). With that in mind, the comprehensive list of goals you create will represent the strategic vision of your household financial situation. The actual financial behaviors each member of the household engages in on a day-to-day basis are the financial tactics that will lead directly to your shared success or failure. The goal of this book—and of your household financial initiatives—is to identify the strategic visions that can motivate and define your financial life, and then to make sense of the tactics that will guide and support you each step of the way. But remember—you'll need to get everyone involved.

If you're married or have a partner, are the two of you in agreement about a shared financial vision of the future? Have you discussed goals and time frames? Do you have a plan to manage money together in pursuit of those goals? It's essential to talk about these things.

If children are in the picture, you'll probably need to remind them—maybe more than once—about what a big difference there is between wanting something and needing something. If Junior's still miffed about not getting his dream car, he might be interested to learn that you'd be happy to have a new car too—but that you're even happier to be setting aside money to help pay for his college tuition instead. He wants a new car—he needs an education. He wants to drive his friends around town—he needs to take the bus.

Help ... I Need Somebody

Don't make the mistake of concerning yourself only with the people inside your household. There may be times when it's prudent to open the door, so to speak, and welcome some outside advice from a qualified professional. This book will teach you the basics about a lot of important financial strategies and options, but at some point you'll probably want or need to work with a fee-only financial professional to determine exactly what consequences your choices might entail. There are potentially complex regulations and considerations surrounding taxes, estate planning, investments, retirement savings, and debt, for example, so it could be prudent to consider hiring someone to help evaluate your situation when the need arises. Ideally, the discussions in the following pages will provide you with the insights you'll need to pick the right type of pro.

Let's see ... Discussing goals. Sharing plans and responsibility. Joining together. Consulting others for assistance. Do you notice a trend here? It really does take all hands to get a grip on household finances. And the key to actually making it happen is communication—talking and thinking together.

But the fact is, a lot of people find it difficult to talk about money—especially if there is stress, fear, or uncertainty involved. If that's the case, why not start by talking about money. There's nothing wrong with saying, "I really feel that we should talk to each other about money and financial security, but to tell you the truth, I feel a bit uncomfortable bringing up the subject at all. However, there are some priorities I think we should discuss, and I wanted to make sure you'd be comfortable doing that."

This approach can be an effective ice breaker, and it also provides people with an opportunity right off the bat to set boundaries, express concerns, etc. Then you can join forces and get to work.

(At the risk of excessive self-promotion, I'd also like to point out that this book can serve as a nice ice breaker and conversational jump starter. "You know, dear, there's a page in *The Standard & Poor's Guide to Personal Finance* that hits the nail right on the head with respect to our XYZ situation. After you take a few minutes to read it, we should talk about our options.")

Don't Fudge It ... Budget

Once you've talked with your family and assembled a list of household goals, you'll need to get busy finding the money to achieve them all. That may be easier said than done, buy you've got to start somewhere, and the best place to begin is almost always your household budget.

But isn't creating and sticking to a budget so ... old-fashioned? It sure is. And there are reasons why the basic strategies of successful budgeting have passed from generation to generation virtually unchanged. The two pillars of budgeting—consistently keeping track of spending and routinely setting aside money for fixed expenses and household goals—will build financial discipline and enhance your ability to achieve important financial objectives.

If you're not already a seasoned budgeter, you'll get the hang of it pretty quickly. In all likelihood, though, the process might seem a bit unsettling at first. You might be unpleasantly surprised to see how much of your spending is unnecessary or poorly planned. But that's no reason to play ostrich and keep your head buried in the sands of financial uncertainty. Creating a budget will help you see the light; sticking to it will help your financial plan take flight.

TABLE 1-1. Budgeting Worksheet

Your income $ _____

Household Spending (Real)		Household Budget (Ideal)	
Mortgage/rent:	$ _____	Mortgage/rent:	$ _____
Insurance:	$ _____	Insurance:	$ _____
Transportation	$ _____	Transportation	$ _____
Groceries	$ _____	Groceries	$ _____
Food at work	$ _____	Food at work	$ _____
Work supplies	$ _____	Work supplies	$ _____
Education	$ _____	Education	$ _____
Phone/utilities	$ _____	Phone/utilities	$ _____
Home maintenance	$ _____	Home maintenance	$ _____
Debt repayment	$ _____	Debt repayment	$ _____
Medical/dental costs	$ _____	Medical/dental costs	$ _____
Clothing	$ _____	Clothing	$ _____
Hobbies/leisure	$ _____	Hobbies/leisure	$ _____
Charity	$ _____	Charity	$ _____
Books/subscriptions	$ _____	Books/subscriptions	$ _____
Other expenses:		Other expenses:	
_____	$ _____	_____	$ _____
_____	$ _____	_____	$ _____
_____	$ _____	_____	$ _____
Spending Total =	$ _____	Budget Total =	$ _____

A Two-Step Program

The budgeting process requires you to make two lists. One, called "Household Spending," identifies where and how everyone in the house actually spends their money on a daily basis. The other, called "Household Budget," identifies how much you should be spending on your ongoing expenses, such as housing costs, utility bills, retirement contributions, etc.

The Household Budget list will show everyone where you need to stand on a monthly basis. If it turns out that you spend less than you earn, congratulations. (Now what are you going to do with the "extra" money?) But if you regularly spend most or all of your income, that's a problem. A potentially huge problem, in fact. In that event, you'd need to take a fresh look at the Household Spending list and find ways to cut back.

Stash Some Cash: The Importance of Emergency Savings

After you've had a chance to get the whole household involved in an effective budgeting campaign, you'll be ready to start pursuing the entire range of financial goals outlined in the following chapters. Before you start thinking about the long term, however, it's essential to prepare for any unexpected emergencies that could put a major strain on your budget with little or no advance warning.

As a rule of thumb, financial professionals typically recommend that you set up a so-called emergency savings account and try to set aside enough money in it to cover all of your routine expenses for three to six months. That might seem like a daunting task, but what other options would you have for dealing with a financial crisis? Think about it: If you or another key earner in your household were to become unemployed tomorrow, where would you find the money to pay for your mortgage/rent, insurance premiums, utilities, and groceries? Hopefully, you'll never find yourself in such a situation, but bad things like that happen to good people all the time. In 2003 alone, for example, more than 1.8 million Americans lost their jobs as part of large-scale layoffs. And you can be sure that there weren't nearly as many "golden parachutes" handed out as pink slips.

Even if you're not worried about being laid off, it's still a good idea to set aside a nice chunk of change for use in emergencies only. After all, life has a way of throwing a curveball when you least expect it. If your place of work were to burn to the ground tonight, would your employer or clients continue to pay you until everything was up and running again?

We live and learn, as the saying goes, but do yourself a favor and learn from the mistakes of others instead of making the same mistake yourself. Use the savings from your newly created household budget to start funding an emergency savings account as soon as possible.

Where to Keep the Money?

Many of us may know people—or have heard stories about people—who lived through the Great Depression and lost everything when their banks went out of business. Since then they've kept all of their money hidden under their mattress.

That's a perfect example of how *not* to handle your emergency savings. Because these days, not only does the Federal Deposit Insurance Corporation insure bank savings accounts, but almost all financial institutions will pay you interest on your savings if you place them in the right type of account.

Before going any further, let's make an important distinction between interest and investment earnings.

Interest represents the essentially risk-free promise by a financial institution to pay you a certain amount of money each year, expressed as a percentage of your account value. For example, if you have $1,000 in a savings account that pays a 3 percent annual interest rate, then the interest payments for that year will amount to $30. (Technically speaking, you could receive more than $30 if the interest payments are made on a prorated, monthly basis, because each monthly payment would have the effect of increasing your account value above $1,000.)

Investment earnings, on the other hand, can be much less predictable (depending on the type of investment), and the pursuit of investment earnings can also come with a risk of losing money (although the extent of the risk depends largely on the type of investment).

We'll talk more about the risk and return potential of investments in Chapters 4, 5, and 6, but in general here's what you need to know: For most people, the best place to stash emergency savings is either in an insured, interest paying savings account or in a low-risk, conservative investment account.

So what does this all have to do with not hiding money under your mattress? A lot. It's up to you to select the right type of account for your emergency savings. But not all bank accounts (or stable value funds or money market funds or CDs) are created equal. So shop around, and be sure to compare not only the rates of return they offer, but also other important characteristics, such as whether those returns are fixed or variable, and whether there are annual fees, check-writing privileges, early withdrawal penalties, etc. Also, keep in mind that not all such accounts are insured.

Finally, you need to consider two more things about creating and funding an emergency savings account. First, don't let your homeowner's (or renter's) insurance policy lull you into a false sense of security. There are some potentially significant expenses they may not cover, such as flood damage. (For more on insurance, see Chapter 12.) Also, once you've accumulated some money in your emergency savings account, give yourself a big pat on the back ... and then do your best to forget the account exists (unless you're ready to add more money). It's for emergencies only, remember? Not Junior's new car.

The financial self-discipline necessary to organize a household financial plan, create a budget, and accumulate emergency savings is something you should be proud of, and it's something that will make it possible for you to effectively pursue other important financial goals in the future, such as aggressively paying off debt, investing for retirement, and preparing to pay for a college education.

CHAPTER 2

Debt and Credit— A Double-Edged Sword

These days it's almost impossible to heed the advice of William Shakespeare, who famously preached, "Neither a borrower nor a lender be."

Well, it's easy enough (for most of us anyway) not to be a lender. But good luck trying to make it from cradle to grave without being a borrower. At some point in life it will probably be necessary—and quite possibly prudent—to borrow money in order to get ahead. For most people, life isn't like a game of Monopoly. You don't start out with all the money you need and then simply try to accumulate more. Quite often, in order to get the big-ticket items you need, you must borrow.

Consider this: According to a report issued by the U.S. Federal Reserve Board in 2003, the median amount of debt among American families borrowing on installment loans, credit cards, and other lines of credit was $15,500. (Median means that half of the families had more debt and half had less.) Strictly speaking, a lot of that debt probably isn't necessary, but it's a fact of life. It's also a fact that debt, when used responsibly, can be a wonderful thing. When used irresponsibly, though, it can threaten or even destroy your long-term financial security.

It's easy to lump debt into one big category, but in reality there are many different types of debt, including:

➤ Revolving credit: A loan that allows you to carry a balance indefinitely in exchange for your making minimum payments on a regular basis, usually monthly. Credit cards, for example, are considered revolving credit accounts.

➤ Mortgage: A loan issued for a fixed amount of time (the "term"), typically for purchasing a home or other property. (The federal tax deductions for home mortgage interest expenses provide a major incentive for owning, rather than renting, your home.)

➤ Home equity loan or credit line: Credit issued to homeowners based on the amount of equity (ownership) they have in their homes.

➤ Bank/credit union loans: Personal or business loans that may require collateral.

The Good

Shakespeare might not have been so quick to issue his famous advice if he'd been able to look into a crystal ball and get a look at the concept—and costs—of the so-called American dream. Simply put, it would be next to impossible for the average American to buy a home and put children through college without borrowing. And when you consider that home ownership represents the greatest single source of wealth for many households—or that college graduates can expect to earn $1 million more during their lifetimes than those who only graduate from high school—it becomes clear that borrowing to achieve some goals can actually be a smart investment in a household's long-term future. But there are also less dramatic examples of how going into debt can help you get ahead—as long as you don't get too carried away. For example, consider the potential benefits of borrowing to buy a car from the perspective of a young graduate on a job search.

Let's assume that Maria is fresh out of college and ready to embark on a career as a fashion consultant (or saleswoman, business owner, etc.). She's been driving her beloved but banged-up 1974 Dodge Dart since high school but knows it won't make the right impression on the type of clients (or employers) she hopes to associate with. And she certainly can't afford to pay cash for a better car right now. But in the big picture, projecting the right professional image and getting started in a career right away could help Maria get ahead in life—by enabling her to pay off student loans ahead of schedule and to start setting aside more money for retirement and other long-term goals.

The solution? Maria applies for a modest car loan from her family's credit union, and uses it to buy a well-maintained, nice-looking used car, which she then drives confidently from one appointment to another. Soon she's earning the kind of money she hoped for, in large part because she used a debt opportunity to make a smart investment in both her short- and long-term future. (Of course, if she'd gone over the top and bought a Ferrari or Porsche, one might not be so quick to sing her praises.)

The Bad

Often, good credit habits go bad not dramatically, but gradually over time. Instead of paying off your credit card balance every month, for instance, you might start to carry a balance from one statement to the next, ringing up interest expenses in the process. And maybe you got into that situation in the first place by gradually changing the way you use your card. Instead of using it only for emergencies or to purchase important, expensive items you intend to pay off right away, perhaps you occasionally used it for daily expenses so you could keep that last $20 bill in your wallet.

Just as a journey of 1,000 miles starts with a single step, the journey toward out-of-control indebtedness often starts with a single decision to use credit for the wrong reasons. And it's not just credit card debt that needs to be managed wisely. Home equity loans, for example, can prove to be a savvy way of increasing a home's value, or can represent just another source of misspent money. Case in point: If you're thinking about selling your house and decide to use a $10,000 home equity loan to renovate the kitchen, then the improvement might increase your asking price by $20,000 or more.

But taking out a home equity loan to finance an expensive vacation wouldn't be nearly as prudent. In other words, debt isn't necessarily a bad thing—rather, it's your decisions about how to use debt that will make or break you.

The Downright Ugly

Ultimately, poor debt management skills could lead to one of the darkest destinations on any financial journey: bankruptcy. We'll talk more about that shortly, but first let's run through some of the warning signs that your (ab)use of debt is getting dangerously out of control:

➤ You're using cash advances from one credit card to make the minimum monthly payment on another credit card.

➤ You can't afford to make all of your minimum payments every month.

➤ You're forced to skip payments on routine household expenses (such as utility bills) in order to make your debt payments.

➤ Your applications for new credit are rejected.

➤ Creditors are calling you to arrange payment of outstanding bills.

Fortunately, there are steps you can take to turn things around before it's too late.

If You Use It, Don't Abuse It

Most of what you've read about debt to this point has been about the potentially positive reasons for borrowing. But it doesn't matter how noble your reasons may be—if you can't repay the debt (or can't repay it fast enough), then you might end up permanently short-changing yourself.

Consider the fact that the money you end up paying on interest is money you'll never see again. But if you were able to invest that money instead, it could grow significantly over the years. Assume you spend $80 each month on interest for five years. Bye-bye, $4,800.

It was nice knowing you. But if you invested that $80 each month in an account earning an 8 percent annual rate of return, you'd have $5,917 in your account after five years, $27,868 after 15 years, $76,589 after 25 years, and $184,734 after 35 years. Not bad, eh?

There is another very good reason for not letting your debt get out of control. Credit reporting agencies (CRAs) compile detailed information on just about anyone who uses—or has used—credit. Whenever you apply for a loan (such as a mortgage), the lender typically requests details of your credit history from one or more CRA in order to evaluate your creditworthiness.

Depending on what your credit history reveals, the lender will either approve or deny your loan application. And if your loan is approved, your credit history is still important because it's likely to affect the interest rate the lender wants you to pay on the debt. But that's not all. Other people—such as potential insurers, landlords, and employers—also have the right to review your credit history. So your decision not to make those minimum monthly payments when money was tight a few years ago might mean that you won't be able to rent that really nice apartment you just found. It might also cause a boss to think twice about hiring or promoting you.

Consider this: A company called ADP compiled data revealing that companies conducted more than 3.7 million background checks on job applicants in 2003—an increase of approximately 26 percent from 2002. And as part of those background checks, 44 percent of all credit record checks revealed negative information about the applicants, such as a court judgment, a lien or bankruptcy, or the fact that an account had been referred to a collection agency. The ADP study didn't examine whether those applicants were negatively influenced by the unflattering information, but it's unlikely to have helped. (You'll learn more about credit reports a bit later.)

To be fair, there can be a fine line between credit use and credit abuse in many households. What you need to do is recognize where that line is ... and vow not to cross it. The following commonsense suggestions concerning big-ticket items, retirement accounts, and maximizing your income might help you rein in your debts before (and after) they start to get out of control.

Downsize Big-Ticket Items

Do you remember the rapper M.C. Hammer, who made—and squandered—a multimillion dollar fortune in the 1990s? By his own admission, one of his biggest financial mistakes was spending way too much money on the home of his dreams. Most of us will probably never be in a position to build a mansion we can't afford, of course, but many of us will eventually face the temptation to finance a car or a home (or a boat or a vacation cottage) that we probably really can't afford.

You might think: Why drive something boring (and affordable) when the salesman on the lot is so eager to arrange a loan for that flashy new coupe or SUV? Or: Why buy a decent house in a respectable neighborhood when you can borrow up to your limit and buy something showier—and pricier—in a trendier part of town, instead?

Because you could dig a debt hole you might not be able to out get of, that's why.

If you've already crossed the line of reasonable spending, don't wait for the hammer to come crashing down on your dreams. Instead, remove your ego from the equation and be honest enough with yourself to make the tough decisions. If you can live with a scaled-down version of your budget-busting home (or car, etc.), then go ahead and do it. It might make sense to sell what you've got (particularly if the price has appreciated) and then acquire a more affordable replacement. And remember, the higher the value of your house (or car), the higher the property (or excise) taxes you pay on it will be each year. So downsizing could increase the amount of cash in your budget right away, and it could also lower your tax bills over the long term.

Avoid Draining Retirement Accounts

One of the basic premises of retirement planning is that you should always contribute as much as you can to tax-friendly retirement accounts and then leave that money alone until you need income during retirement. However, in some cases you may be able to borrow from your account or take an early "hardship distribution" from a workplace plan. If you have the right to get money early, do yourself a favor and don't do it. The longer you leave the money in there, the more secure your long-term future may be.

If you are tempted, though, at least be sure that you understand the rules—and the long-term financial consequences—before acting. Most 401(k) plan loans usually impose competitive interest rates, and those interest payments also go right back into your own account. In other words, you're essentially borrowing from yourself. On the other hand, if you leave the company before the debt is repaid, you'll need to repay the entire amount within 60 days. Failure to do so would result in income taxes and a 10 percent early withdrawal penalty on the amount outstanding. Also, many plans don't allow you to keep contributing until you've repaid the loan, so not only have you borrowed against your current savings, but you're also delaying further contributions. A hardship withdrawal (also called a hardship distribution) doesn't require repayment, but once the money is gone from your account, it's gone for good.

In either case, a loan or a withdrawal is likely to result in an "opportunity cost" or "investment opportunity cost." That's because the money you take out of the account reduces the potential investment growth of the account. The less money you have in the account, even temporarily, the less your potential investment earnings will be. Over the long term, that lost opportunity could carry a big price tag.

Try to Maximize Income

A lot of the people reading this book are probably already doing everything in their power to earn as much income as possible. These days, it's not at all uncommon for both parents in a household to work at least one job each, and even then money is often still tight. But a lot of Americans are dangerously deep in debt and not doing enough to solve the problem. The Declaration of Independence promises each of us the right to "life, liberty, and the pursuit of happiness," but those goals aren't a substitute for hard work; rather, they're usually a reward for hard work.

Modern society, with all its conveniences and stresses, seems to have convinced some of us that leisure time is a right, not a privilege. But if debt is a problem that your current income can't solve, it may be necessary to work more—if only for a while. And there's nothing wrong with that. Working harder or longer than average isn't something to be ashamed of; it's something to be proud of. In fact, that type of industriousness is what helped make the United States such a powerful economic force in the first place.

For reasons that probably don't have much to do with financial discipline, some people may still worry that others perceive their "moonlighting" as a sign of financial weakness. In reality, though, that willingness to toil rather than relax can make the difference between struggling with debt or wiping it off the books once and for all.

So maybe you have some debt, but you don't want to downsize the house, sell your perfectly good car, or take a second job. Fair enough. Here are some less radical ideas for freeing up the cash that will help you get out of debt.

➤ Cut two or three discretionary (as opposed to mandatory) items out of your budget. Don't renew the subscription to that magazine you only skim through. Stop spending money on fancy coffee drinks during the week; even once or twice a day might be too much. Multiply two four-dollar trips to the coffee shop by 200 work days a year, and you're looking at a $1,600 annual coffee-break bill—with nothing to show for it but a case of the jitters.

➤ Stop using your credit cards. Period. If you can't afford to pay cash for something you want, then don't reach for the plastic.

➤ Avoid late fees by paying bills on time.

➤ Use a "windfall" (such as a bonus from work, a tax refund, or an inheritance) to pay off debt.

➤ Shop for bargains, even if you need to travel a bit farther to find them. For example, if you live in the city, you might want to do some of your shopping in the suburbs. Groceries, household items, auto mechanics, and possibly even veterinarians might all be less expensive once you get away from the high-rent district.

Why the Minimum Payment Isn't Enough

If you want to learn exactly how creditors (such as credit card issuers) calculate the amount of your minimum monthly payments, read the fine print on the back of your account statement or on the paperwork you received after opening the account. In most cases, you'll find that the minimum payment represents a specific percentage of your total debt—usually a fairly small percentage. This is because creditors are in the business of making money by collecting the interest debtors owe them. The lower the payment you make each month, the longer you'll be in debt—and thus the more you'll owe in interest, and the more money the credit card company makes off of you.

And remember, not all of your payment reduces your debt—some of that money is the interest you're being charged (which becomes the profit the creditor is making from doing business with you). So, the higher your interest rates, the less debt (also called principal) you pay off with each minimum payment. Again, this is another reason to read the fine print on your account statement—to see how much of your payment actually goes toward reducing your debt. If you're required to pay a $200 minimum payment and $140 of that $200 is earmarked for interest, then you're only paying off $60 of the principal. The rest goes straight to the creditor's bottom line. And, of course, new interest charges continue to be added to your total bill if you carry a balance into the next billing period.

What does that mean for you? It could mean that you're essentially throwing good money after bad, caught in a vicious cycle of making minimum payments that barely outpace the effect of potentially crippling interest charges.

One way to break out of the minimum monthly payment trap is to stop charging new purchases on the card and to repay the debt as aggressively as possible. Remember, the minimum payment system wasn't designed to help your financial situation, but to improve the creditor's financial situation at your expense. To beat creditors at their own game, you've got to consistently give them more money than they're asking for. Instead of paying just the minimum, send in as much as you can possibly afford.

When it comes to debt, interest rates take top priority. Later in this chapter you'll find some strategies and considerations related to improving your debt situation by consolidating your high-interest debts into a single low-rate account. And if you anticipate the need to apply for a new, and cheaper, line of credit, it's critical to maintain a healthy credit history

Of course, there will always be people who have a hard time making even the minimum payments, never mind paying more than the minimum. If you're in that position, and you work for a company that offers "direct deposit" of pay into your bank account, it might be a good idea to sign up as part of your debt repayment strategy. Many credit card companies will allow you to establish an automatic payment arrangement, in which your monthly payment is transferred directly from your checking account. And if direct deposit can help impose the financial discipline necessary for an aggressive attack on debt, why wouldn't you sign up to take advantage of it? By picking a date on or near your payday that the credit card payments will be made, such as the fifteenth or thirtieth of each month, you can guarantee that your money will go where it needs to before you withdraw and spend it elsewhere.

And let's not forget the most obvious way to get your credit card payments under control, even more obvious than transferring balances to lower-rate accounts and doubling up on your monthly payments: Stop using the cards. Cut them up if you need to. Or put them in a watertight plastic bag and freeze them in an even bigger bag of water, so they're eventually encased in a block of ice that you'll only thaw out in the kitchen sink while sleeping on your decision to use them again. Whatever it takes, hit the brakes and stop allowing credit card spending to drive you ever deeper into debt.

It still might take a while to pay off your debts, but keep plugging away. You'll feel good about doing the right thing, and the financial habits and discipline you develop in the process will continue to serve you well long after you've wiped the debt slate clean. Maybe your old "financial personality" made it easy to turn a blind eye to debt and the serious long-term problems it can cause. So what? That was then, this is now. The new you is always serious about eliminating household debt once and for all.

Your Credit History: What You Don't Know Could Hurt You

Now let's take an even closer look at the significance of your credit history. First of all, it's important to understand that CRAs (credit reporting agencies) acquire and sell four types of information about consumers:

➤ Personal identification and employment information, such as your name, date of birth, Social Security number, current and previous addresses, and current and previous employers

➤ Account information, including details of current and previous credit accounts, how much credit was extended to you, whether you have a history of late payments, and any credit-related "events," such as the referral of an overdue account to a collections agency

➤ Inquiries about your credit history, including a list of all creditors who have reviewed your file during the past year, and the names of any people or businesses that have reviewed your credit history within the past two years for employment purposes

➤ Public record information, such as details of bankruptcy, liens, and civil judgments against you

Whenever someone reviews your credit history ("runs a credit check"), this is the information they will review for insights about who you are and how you handle financial responsibilities. Unfortunately, any negative information that appears in your credit history doesn't go away as quickly as you'd like. In most cases, CRAs can report negative information for seven years, but in some cases it will stay on your record even longer.

For example, information about criminal convictions can be reported forever. Bankruptcies can stay on file for 10 years. Details of lawsuits or unpaid judgments against you can remain on your credit history for seven years or until the statute of limitations expires (whichever is longer). And there is no time limit on information related to an application for a job paying more than $75,000, or related to an application for credit or life insurance valued at $150,000 or more.

Keep in mind, however, that routine credit checks shouldn't be confused with what the Federal Trade Commission refers to as "investigative consumer reports," which are even more thorough than regular credit checks and usually used to evaluate applicants for employment or insurance. As part of an investigative consumer report, your neighbors or associates may be interviewed about your reputation, lifestyle, and personality traits. If you are the subject of such an investigation, you have the right to ask for information about the report, but the CRAs are not required to identify the sources of the information they have collected.

One thing that doesn't appear on your credit report is your "credit score." That's because creditors purchase and analyze information provided by CRAs and then assign a credit score as a way of impartially grading your creditworthiness. Creditors do this by using statistical programs that evaluate the credit "performance" of other consumers who share your financial characteristics. Based on the creditor's understanding of how other people in your situation have typically managed their debts in the past, the creditor will assign you a specific credit score. While this may seem impersonal, creditors like the fact that credit scoring allows them to make calculated, consistent, and objective business decisions. There's a catch, though: Different creditors use different scoring programs, so results may vary from lender to lender.

If you were denied credit, you're entitled to receive a free copy of your credit report. You should also ask the creditor who denied you what factors influenced the decision and how you might be able to improve your credit score. Also, remember that too many applications for new credit could actually lower your credit score. Some people think that's just a myth, but it's not. It's true. (However, credit checks performed without your knowledge, such as those conducted by creditors "prescreening" potential customers, will not count against you.)

Financial decisions that damage your credit history can make it more expensive—if not impossible—to get credit again. But, beware: Credit reporting mistakes can and do happen. You might have every reason to believe that you have perfect credit, but if your credit file contains any errors, creditors will probably assume the information is correct and may decide that you're a bad credit risk. Because of that, you should consider obtaining a copy of your credit report every year to verify the information.

And here's something else to consider for anyone who has ever been through a divorce. If you and your ex haven't closed the joint credit accounts you had, then your names—and credit files—may still be linked (even though you're not). In other words, if your ex ends up destroying his or her credit after the divorce, you could get dragged down, too. Kind of makes you want to contact the CRAs and review your credit report, doesn't it?

Now you can see why the title of this chapter refers to debt as a "double-edged sword"—because borrowing can ultimately make your financial life much better or much worse. The deciding factor, of course, is you. So if you must borrow, proceed with caution and try to repay the debt as soon as possible.

CHAPTER 3

Your Rights and Responsibilities as a Credit Consumer

So there it is: The government allows private companies to buy and sell your personal financial data—data that may be unflattering and possibly even incorrect. And based on that information, you could be denied a job, a promotion, a loan, an insurance policy, or even an apartment. But just as businesses have certain rights related to your credit files, so do you. There are no laws requiring you to obtain and verify the accuracy of your credit report, but there are federal laws that give you the right to do exactly that. And you'd be wise to exercise those rights at least once a year.

The main federal law that defines and protects consumer credit rights is known as the Fair Credit Reporting Act, or FCRA for short. The Federal Trade Commission is the government agency that enforces the FCRA. The FTC does not promise that every consumer will be able to get credit, but it does protect your rights to a "fair and equal opportunity" to be considered for credit and to settle disputes arising from credit reporting errors. You have six key rights under the FCRA:

1. You have the right to obtain a current copy of your credit report containing all of the information that was in your file when you requested it.

2. You have the right to learn the names of anyone who obtained a copy of your credit report in the past year (or past two years for employment purposes).

3. If a company denies your application based on information provided by a CRA, you have the right to receive from the company the name and address of the CRA that provided the information.

4. You have the right to request a free copy of your credit report within 60 days of a denied application, as long as the application was denied because of information provided by the CRA.

5. You have the right to dispute incomplete or inaccurate information on your credit report. Both the CRA and the original source of the disputed information are required to investigate and respond to your challenge.

6. If a dispute is not settled in your favor, you have the right to tell your side of the story by adding a written explanation of the situation to your credit file. Whoever reviews your credit record in the future will still see the information you unsuccessfully challenged, but they will also see your side of things too.

Another federal law, the Equal Credit Opportunity Act (ECOA), makes it illegal for creditors to discriminate against applicants on the basis of age, marital status, national origin, public assistance income, race, religion, or gender.

Any business that extends credit or plays a role in credit decisions—including banks, credit card companies, credit unions, private loan and finance companies, real estate brokers, and retail establishments—must adhere to the ECOA.

The FCRA and ECOA are the two pillars of consumer-debt rights, but there are a few more laws worth noting too. The Fair Credit Billing Act (FCBA) and the Electronic Fund Transfers Act (EFTA) spell out the rights and procedures available to those who have problems with their credit billing or electronic fund transfers, such as charges for purchases you did not make, incorrect dates or amounts on account statements, etc. (If you're not already in the habit of regularly reviewing all of your financial records for accuracy and thoroughness, then get in the habit starting now.)

In addition, the Fair Debt Collections Act (FDCA) protects you from annoying debt collectors. Actually, the FDCA doesn't completely prevent them from hounding you, but it does place limits on that hounding. Ultimately, of course, it's your own job to protect yourself from debt collectors by not getting into debt trouble in the first place. But if you do get into trouble, it's good to know that the FDCA establishes these guidelines and rights:

➤ Debt collectors cannot contact you before 8:00 A.M. or after 9:00 P.M.

➤ Debt collectors cannot contact you at work if they know your employer does not allow them to do so.

➤ Debt collectors cannot harass you or abuse you.

➤ Debt collectors cannot lie to you, such as telling you that failure to pay a bill is a crime if in fact it is not.

➤ Debt collectors must identify themselves by name when they contact you on the telephone.

➤ Debt collectors are required to cease contacting you after receiving that request from you in writing.

To be fair, many debt collectors are decent, hardworking people who abide by all of the rules that govern their profession. They earn their living by contacting people who are not paying their debts, and by helping creditors try to recover money that is owed to them. Shooting the messenger isn't going to solve your problems. What's more, being contacted by a debt collector should be considered a red-flag event in every household. It means that you're either responsible for an unpaid bill, or a creditor thinks you're responsible for an unpaid bill. Either way, it could hurt your credit report, and hiding from the problem might only make it worse. Talk to the debt collector—and the creditor, if necessary—to arrange a solution as quickly as possible.

Get Your Credit Reports Here!

It's easy enough to check your personal financial records—all you need to do is carefully read each of your monthly account statements (including the fine print on the back). Checking your credit report will take a little more work, but it's still pretty easy to do, so you shouldn't be intimidated by it. You do it by contacting at least one of the three big national CRAs and following the procedures for getting a copy of your credit report:

Equifax
(800) 685-1111
www.equifax.com

Experian
(888) 397-3742
www.experian.com

TransUnion
(800) 916-8800
www.transunion.com

The most anyone will be required to pay for their credit report is nine dollars, but thanks to a recently enacted law, U.S. consumers are now entitled to receive a free copy of their credit reports from Equifax, Experian, and TransUnion once every 12 months (effective nationwide as of September 1, 2005). You may also have the right to receive a free credit report if:

➤ You were denied or were the subject of a negative action related to credit, a job application, insurance, or a government license or benefit because of information in your credit file. You must request the credit report within 60 days of the negative decision.

➤ You were denied a home or apartment rental or were charged a higher than usual deposit. Again, you must request the report within 60 days.

➤ You can prove that you are unemployed and plan to seek employment within 60 days.

➤ You receive public assistance.

➤ You can certify that fraud may have resulted in the appearance of incorrect information on your credit report.

By the way, a friendly word of warning: Although CRAs are indeed required to provide credit reports to consumers as outlined above, they also sell other credit-related packages, such as credit monitoring services, credit scores, and monthly credit updates. And sometimes the price for these is significantly higher than the nine-dollar (maximum) fee they charge for a basic credit report. If you really want this extra information, it's there for you. But there's a good chance you can get everything you need for just nine dollars or less. Just don't be surprised if you visit a CRA's Web site and discover that it's much easier to locate information about how to order the pricier packages than the less expensive option. Don't be tricked into making an unnecessary purchase.

Once you get your credit reports, you'll see that each CRA presents the same general information in slightly different formats. That's not important. What is important is whether any negative information appears on your report, and whether that information is accurate. Read the instructions that explain how to interpret each report so you don't accidentally overlook any subtle details. Pay particular attention to the symbols or notations each CRA uses to highlight accounts with negative information.

Also, don't assume that each CRA will show identical account information. I checked my credit reports several years ago and discovered that one of the CRAs was mistakenly reporting negative information, but the other two were not. If I had only checked one of my credit reports instead of all three, there's a one-in-three chance I would have missed the damaging information.

I followed the instructions that came with that particular credit report and wrote a letter to the CRA explaining why I felt the erroneous information should be removed from my file. A month or so later that CRA informed me that it had honored my request and removed the negative information. There were no conversations, confrontations, or heated discussions—nobody even contacted me until I got the news I was hoping for. Since then I've been a vocal advocate of reviewing and, if necessary, challenging credit reports.

The paperwork you receive with your credit report should contain information about how to challenge an item that appears on your file. Also, the FTC's Web site (www.ftc.gov) contains a recommended format that you should use when writing your letter.

The CRA must respond to your request for a reinvestigation within 30 days and must forward your information about the dispute to the business or agency that originally reported the negative information in question. At that point the information provider must look into your claims and report its findings to the CRA. If the process results in a change to your credit report, the CRA must provide you with the results of the reinvestigation and a free copy of your updated credit report. The CRA is also obligated to inform anyone who has received your credit report within the past six months of the changes. And you can also request the CRA to send an updated version to anyone who received one within the past two years for employment purposes.

Credit Repair: If It Sounds Too Good to Be True, It Probably Is

Considering how important it is to have a good credit history, you can be sure that some people would probably go to great lengths to improve their own less-than-perfect files. After all, maintaining good credit could save you thousands and thousands of dollars over the years as a result of the lower interest rates you'd qualify to pay on credit cards, car loans, mortgages, etc.

Unfortunately, there is no way for you to legitimately repair a damaged credit file. If the information is accurate, it stays there. "But wait," you might say. "What about those ads on cable TV and the Internet promising to repair my credit for a fee?" Unless they've discovered a perfectly legitimate credit repair strategy that even the FTC doesn't know about, you should be wary. Because the only things that will legally heal a damaged credit report are time and debt repayment.

For the most part, companies that solicit payments for credit repair services are a waste of money at best, and possibly even downright fraudulent at worst. The people who run these companies know how desperate some people are to improve their credit, and they prey on that desperation. There is nothing legal that a so-called credit repair service can do for you for a fee that you can't do for yourself for free. Some such agencies may even encourage you to break the law as part of a crooked scheme they've devised. For all those reasons, you're almost certainly better off avoiding credit repair businesses altogether. Here are several signs that should make you suspicious of businesses offering credit repair services:

> They require you to pay an up-front fee.

> They try to discourage you from contacting legitimate credit agencies.

> They encourage you to declare that accurate information on your credit report is inaccurate and should be removed.

> They promise to provide you with a "new identity" (usually by misusing a Social Security number or Employer Identification Number).

Although you can't miraculously erase bad memories from a credit report, there are less dramatic steps you can take to potentially improve your overall credit profile. For example, if you were denied credit because you have no credit history or an insufficient credit file, you may be able to have previously unreported positive information added to your file, such as details about accounts with your credit union or local businesses. If you want this information to appear on your credit report, you may need to ask the creditor to provide it to the CRAs.

Another way to maintain a healthy credit report is to contact creditors about potential problems before it's too late. If you know that you might have trouble paying a bill, contact the creditor before the due date and try to arrange something that works for both of you. Your credit report may show that you negotiated a repayment arrangement, but that may reflect better on you than having a creditor refer your account to a collection agency. Creditors want you to repay them, and it costs them money to hire debt collectors. If you call a creditor with the sincere intention of fulfilling your financial responsibilities, you might find a receptive audience.

Real World Strategies

When you get right down to it, there are two general rules that should guide your thinking about debt.

Rule 1: Don't get in over your head by accumulating more debt than you need and can afford.

Rule 2: If you beak Rule 1, act fast to get back on track before the debt inflicts long-term damage on your financial well-being.

If you're lucky, an aggressive repayment strategy, such as doubling up on your minimum monthly payment, will be enough to get you out of the red. If your debt has become unmanageable, though, there are a few other strategies to consider, ranging from working with a nonprofit debt counselor, to consolidating existing debts with a new, less expensive loan, all the way to (gulp) declaring bankruptcy.

Debt Counseling

Until fairly recently, most nonprofit debt counseling agencies helped consumers by providing free financial and budgeting advice, by negotiating lower interest rates with creditors, and by establishing debt management plans (DMPs). Such services were often available free of charge to the consumer or for a low fee. Instead of earning their money from the debtors they advised, debt counselors typically received most of their funding from the credit card companies. But that's been changing in recent years, and not necessarily for the better.

According to a 2003 report by the Consumer Federation of American (CFA) and the National Consumer Law Center (NCLC), credit card companies historically paid the counselors 15 percent of the debt that the counselors helped them recover through the DMPs.

Unfortunately, that's not always the case anymore. Many creditors have stopped offering lower interest rates to debtors enrolled in DMPs, and some have even raised interest rates for DMP partici- pants. And instead of paying 15 percent to the counseling agencies, creditors today often pay just 8 percent or less.

As a result, the CFA/NCLC announced that a "new generation" of debt counselors now poses a "severe threat to consumers" by charg- ing excessive fees, offering improper advice, advocating "deceptive practices," and by generally abusing their nonprofit status. And debtors seem to have taken notice. According to the CFA/NCLC report, consumer complaints to the Better Business Bureau have sky- rocketed since the new breed of credit counseling agencies started to claim a bigger share of the marketplace—from just 261 complaints filed in 1998 to 1,480 in 2002.

In an ideal world, a debt counseling professional would spend a good deal of time reviewing every aspect of your financial situation and then make suggestions about ways you could more efficiently use your available resources to get out of debt. If discipline alone wouldn't do the trick, then the counselor might encourage you to enroll in a DMP.

DMPs historically worked like this: You agreed to stop using and applying for credit, and the counseling agency would agree to nego- tiate with creditors on your behalf to reduce late fees and interest rates and to arrange a repayment schedule. Then, instead of paying various creditors yourself, you would make just one monthly pay- ment to the counseling agency, which would then divvy up the money among your creditors.

Unfortunately, not all debt counselors operate like that these days. For example, some credit counseling agencies allegedly fail to make those payments on time or fail to fully and honestly disclose their fees to consumers. In some cases the fees they charge are exorbi- tant—sometimes totaling hundreds of dollars just to enroll in a DMP. And some skip the counseling services altogether, offering only for- fee DMP services even when they may not be necessary.

But that doesn't mean all credit counseling agencies should be avoided. Some are indeed legitimate, have your best interests at heart, and operate in the "ideal world" manner previously described.

So how can you tell the good from the bad? For starters, don't assume that all advertising is accurate and honest. If possible, get referrals from trusted family, friends, or associates who have worked with debt counselors. Also, check with the BBB to learn whether the agencies you're considering have been the subject of consumer complaints. Once you've narrowed down the search, contact each agency and ask the following questions:

➤ What services do they offer in addition to DMPs?

➤ What fees, if any, will you be required to pay?

➤ Will you receive a written agreement or contract?

➤ What qualifications do the counselors possess?

➤ What would happen if you were unable to make a full monthly payment?

To make matters easier from the get-go, you might want to start your search in familiar territory. Universities, the military, and credit unions, for example, might offer free or low-priced debt counseling services to members of the organization and their families. Regardless of which agency you're considering, look out for these red flags identified by the CFA/NCLC:

➤ High fees (more than about $50 to set up a DMP, and monthly fees exceeding about $25)

➤ Pressure to pay "voluntary" fees that you can't afford

➤ A "hard sell" focusing exclusively on consolidation loans

➤ Employees who are paid by commission (a sign that the company may be more interested in its own financial well-being than yours)

➤ Agencies that recommend a DMP after less than 20 or 30 minutes of consultation

➤ Agencies that offer only DMPs and no educational services, such as personal finance classes or budgeting advice

Two more points to remember: Credit counselors can't do anything to remove accurate, negative information from your credit report, no matter how much you pay them. And the fact that you've worked with a debt counselor might appear on your credit report. Some lenders might be turned off by that information, but others could see it as a good sign.

Debt Consolidation

Credit counseling agencies often advise consumers to consolidate their existing debts by taking a new, low-interest loan and then using that money to repay their various high-interest loans. With a debt consolidation loan, the principal amount of your debt stays the same, but your interest expenses can drop dramatically, or disappear altogether if you're able to open a new account charging zero interest on transferred balances. As an added bonus, you'll only have one account, so you'll have less paperwork to manage and fewer checks to write each month.

But consider yourself warned: There may be potential drawbacks related to debt consolidation strategies that shouldn't be overlooked. For example, choosing a consolidation loan simply because it offers the lowest monthly payments could mean that you get stuck with a high-rate, long-term loan. Also, cards offering low-interest or zero percent "introductory" rates may impose much higher interest rates after the brief "introductory period" has ended. And you should read the fine print to find out whether there is a fee for transferring balances. You might be required to pay a flat fee or a percentage of the balance you transfer. Finally, it could be risky to consolidate with an otherwise attractive, tax-deductible home equity loan, since you could lose your home if you fail to make the scheduled payments.

If you think a debt consolidation loan would be the most prudent way to improve your financial situation, be sure to do your homework before making a final decision. Again, read all of the fine print and make sure you understand every detail of the loan agreement, particularly those explaining fees and interest rates.

Here's a hypothetical example, outlined in Table 3-1, of how one person—let's call her Robyn—improved her financial health with a debt consolidation loan.

Robyn started out with three different debts amounting to $10,000—a $4,000 credit card balance with an 18 percent interest rate, a $4,000 car loan with five years remaining on the term and a 10 percent interest rate, and a $2,000 balance on a second credit card, charging 15 percent. Assuming (for the sake of simplicity) that Robyn spent $150 each month on credit card payments ($100 for the 18 percent card and $50 for the 15 percent card), it would have taken her a little more than five years to repay all three debts, and it would have cost her about $4,000 in combined interest costs. However, Robyn decided instead to consolidate her debt by taking out a five-year, $10,000 loan charging 10 percent interest. As a result, she was out of debt slightly sooner but also much less expensively. Her average monthly payments were lower, and her total interest expenses were just under $2,645—a savings of about $1,360 overall, or more than $270 annually.

TABLE 3-1. Example of Debt Consolidation

Before consolidation:

$4,000 credit card debt charging 18%
$4,000 car loan charging 10%
$2,000 credit card charging 15%
Time needed to repay: 5+ years
Interest costs = about $4,000

After consolidation:

$10,000 loan charging 10%
Time needed to repay: 5 years
Interest costs = about $2,645

Bankruptcy

Despite all of the strategies available to help manage and eliminate household debt, more than a million Americans reached the conclusion in 2003 that the only way to stop drowning in debt was to declare personal bankruptcy. On one hand, bankruptcy allows creditors to get at least some of the money they're owed, and it allows debtors to wipe the slate clean (sort of) by "discharging" the debts they can't afford to pay. On the other hand, as you read earlier, a bankruptcy will stay on your credit report for up to 10 years, and probably make it more difficult for you to borrow again in the future. Also, there are certain debts that may not be removed by declaring bankruptcy, such as those related to alimony, child support, student loans, and taxes.

Once an individual determines that bankruptcy is the only solution, the next question that needs to be answered is: What type of bankruptcy filing makes more sense, Chapter 7 or Chapter 13? (The well-known Chapter 11 is an option for businesses, not individuals.)

Chapter 7 bankruptcy involves surrendering your property to a court-appointed bankruptcy trustee, who is then responsible for selling those assets to repay your creditors. Laws vary from state to state, but you may be allowed to keep some property if it's deemed to be essential for the support of your household. After your creditors have received the payments mandated by the court, you may be able to retain any money you earn or property you receive in the future.

Chapter 13 bankruptcy lets you hold onto your assets, but future income must be used to repay creditors (again, via a bankruptcy trustee). Chapter 13 is not available to those who owe more than $750,000 in secured debt (i.e., debt that has been "secured" by collateral, such as a home mortgage or car loan) or more than $250,000 in unsecured debt (such as credit card debt).

In either scenario, there are formal procedures that must be followed, such as providing written details of your financial situation to the bankruptcy court, meeting with a bankruptcy trustee, and possibly sitting down with creditors during that meeting. For those reasons—and because bankruptcy laws can be quite complex—it's generally considered a smart move to hire an experienced bankruptcy attorney to steer you through the process and represent you in court. Before hiring anyone, though, request an initial, free consultation. Ask the lawyer what your options are, how much he or she charges, and whether he or she has extensive experience representing other people in similar circumstances.

Of course, you should never let your borrowing get out of control in the first place. But if it happens, remember that bankruptcy is a big deal indeed. Only consider it as an absolute last resort. Instead, try to adhere to the other strategies you read about in this chapter (as well as those found in the other chapters) in order to get yourself on the right track for good.

CHAPTER 4

Investing
Insights

As soon as you start budgeting and getting your debt under control, you'll be in a much better position to pursue other long-term goals, many of which will require you to invest money with the intention of seeing it "grow" over time. With that in mind, this is an appropriate time to talk about the word "asset."

According to the American Heritage Dictionary, an asset is "a useful or valuable quality, person, or thing … a resource." In a general financial sense, "assets" refers to your money and property. If a financial advisor were to ask for a comprehensive list of your assets, he or she would want to see a list (including the dollar value) of your financial accounts, investments, real estate, valuable possessions, and so on. Net worth, on the other hand, is the value of your assets minus the value of your debts.

In the world of investing, the word "assets" has an even more specific meaning. It refers to the stock, bond, and "cash-equivalent"/money market investments that an individual owns. It should come as no surprise, then, to learn that stock, bond, and cash investments are collectively referred to as the three main "asset classes" or "asset categories." Let's take a closer look at each.

Stocks

Stocks represent ownership in a company. For example, if a company worth $10 million has issued 1 million stocks, each individual stock would be worth $10. If you spent $1 million to purchase

100,000 "shares" of stock, you would own exactly 10 percent of the company. By the same token, if you spent $10 to buy just one stock, you would own one one-millionth of that company. Stocks are also called "shares"—because they allow investors to share in the ownership of a company. They're also called "equities," because equity means ownership. For the most part, people invest in stocks because they hope the value of the company will increase, thereby increasing the value of their investment. Here's how that works:

If a company is doing well—or appears poised to do well—then investors are likely to want to own its stock. But stock prices aren't written in stone. Stocks are constantly bought and sold on the stock market, and their prices typically rise or fall depending on supply and demand. So if the company with the $10 share price seems to have a bright future—for instance, by delivering or appearing poised to deliver strong profits—then more investors are going to want to share in that good fortune. As a result, they'll probably "bid up" the price by offering to pay more than $10 per share.

That's right: The potential for better corporate profits can actually push up the value of a company even before anyone sees a penny of those profits. And it can work the other way too. If a company announces potential bad news—such as lower profit forecasts, a big lawsuit, or the departure of key managers—investors might not be willing to pay the current price anymore, and the value of the stock may decline. Again, that could happen even before the potential bad news affects the company. Professional investors might not like to hear it, but for the reasons just described, investors are often described as being motivated by one of two emotions: greed or fear.

That's not entirely fair, of course. The stock market does have a proven long-term track record of delivering generally positive returns over time, despite the short-term ups and downs that sometimes occur between "winning" years. In fact, millions of Americans invest in stocks not because they're inherently greedy people, but rather because they know that stock investments are likely to grow in value over time, enabling them to eventually sell at a profit and use the proceeds to pay for important goals they might not otherwise have been able to afford, such as a college education or a leisurely retirement.

Okay, everything you just read about stocks is true, but it's also a bit oversimplified.

For example, investor demand does influence the value of stock investments, but there are other factors that can influence the value of your stock portfolio. (Portfolio simply means "investment account.") Consider the decision a company makes about how to use its profits.

Basically, a company can do several things with its profits, such as spend them on resources that will improve the business or pay the money back to shareholders in the form of dividend payments. When a company decides to make dividend payments, shareholders basically have two options: They can either receive the dividends as income or automatically reinvest the value of their dividend payments back into the company by using that money to purchase additional stocks.

Assume that you own 1,000 shares of stock priced at $10 per share. If the company announces a dividend payment of $.50 per share, you could either choose to receive $500 in dividend income (1,000 shares multiplied by $.50 per share) or you could reinvest the dividend payment by purchasing an additional 50 shares of stock ($500 dividend divided by $10 per share). Just don't forget that dividend payments are taxable, regardless of how you choose to receive them. Whether you take the cash or buy more stocks, Uncle Sam expects you to pay taxes on the value of the dividends you received.

But there's a lot more to understanding different types of stocks than simply knowing whether the company pays dividends. Just as no two companies are exactly alike, no two stock investments can be expected to share identical characteristics and performance potential. In general, stocks are grouped into several categories based on their issuing companies' size, location, business specialty, financial characteristics, and price performance. Such categories include:

Company Size, or Market Cap

Publicly traded companies—those companies that make their stock available to the general public on the stock market—are often described in terms of their size. This doesn't refer to the actual size of a company's physical facilities, but rather, to its overall dollar value. What's more, when professional investors discuss a company's size, they don't refer to that company's "dollar value" but to its "market capitalization"—"market cap" for short—which essentially means the same thing. Market cap is determined by multiplying a company's current share price by the number of shares on the market. A company with 1 million shares trading at $10 per share would have a market cap of $10 million. If the share price were to rise to $14, the market cap would rise accordingly, to $14 million.

The Investment Company Institute defines a "small-cap" company as having a market cap of $1.6 billion or less. A large cap is defined as being worth at least $10 billion. And a "mid cap" falls into the middle range. If a company's share price rises (or falls) enough, the company could end up in a different market-cap category. For example, a successful small-cap company could eventually become a mid cap, and after that, a large cap.

What's the point of all this market-cap talk? Well, in general, stocks within the same market-cap category may be likely to share some of the same broad characteristics, which can be helpful to know. Two small-cap stocks, for example, might be issued by different types of companies (such as a software maker and a publishing company) but from a financial point of view may have more in common with each other than with large-cap companies in their same line of business. While there may be exceptions to the rules, it's generally safe to describe the different market-cap categories as follows:

➤ Small-cap stocks are often issued by relatively small and/or new companies with limited track records, financial resources, or market share. For those reasons, and because small caps may not be followed closely by investment analysts, their stock prices might have a relatively high degree of volatility (price swings). But though small caps are typically considered riskier investments than large caps, they may also provide investors with greater potential for significant increases in share price. Also, instead of paying dividends to shareholders, small-cap companies are more likely to spend any profits in order to improve the chances of future corporate success, perhaps by hiring new employees or purchasing new equipment.

> Large-cap stocks are typically issued by well-established and/or highly regarded companies. In theory, large caps don't entail as much short-term volatility as small caps, but they also aren't as likely to rise in value as dramatically. Also, because large caps may be on more solid financial ground than small caps, they're more likely to pay dividends to shareholders. For these reasons, large caps may be particularly attractive to investors who desire investment stability and predictability more than a high-risk pursuit of potentially dramatic price increases.

> Mid-cap stocks fall in the middle of the risk/return spectrum. While they may involve less risk and less potential for price appreciation than small caps, they may also be riskier and more likely to grow in value than large caps.

Growth and Value Stocks

Any company—regardless of size—with a stock price that's expected to rise significantly in the future can be described as a "growth" investment, but that label is also sometimes used to describe small, growing companies. On the other hand, stocks of companies that have fallen from favor—or haven't yet reached their potential and therefore are trading at what may be a bargain price—are called "value" stocks. For example, if the price of a stock falls dramatically, some investors might think the company has lost its appeal and they'll avoid buying its stock. But a "value" investor might see an opportunity to buy the stock now, confident that the company will turn things around and the share price will rise again in the future.

The risk of investing in a growth stock is that most of the company's growth may have already taken place, and its share price already may be at its peak. The risk of value investing is that a company's share price may never take off—again or for the first time. Either way, the universal risk of investing in *any* type of company is buying when the share price is high and still owning the stock after the price has fallen below your purchase price. In other words, the primary risk of stock investing is buying high, selling low ... and losing money. (Obviously, the primary appeal of stock investing is the idea of buying low, selling high ... and making money.)

Stock Splits

When a company wants to increase the number of stocks available to investors, it can choose to "split" its existing shares by multiplying their number by a particular factor and by reducing their value in direct proportion.

For example, if our hypothetical $10 million company with 1 million $10 shares on the market announced a two-for-one stock split, its investors would suddenly own twice as many shares at half the price. So instead of owning 100,000 shares at $10 each (worth $1 million), you would own 200,000 shares at $5 each (still worth $1 million). Again, this is a potentially oversimplified example, because a company's decision to split stock could cause investors to push the share price up or down, in which case your $1 million investment would be worth more or less than $1 million.

Common and Preferred Stocks

One more thing: There are two different types of stock. "Common stock" (or "common shares") is what people are usually referring to when they talk about stocks. "Preferred stock" ("preferred shares") is similar to common stock, but typically pays out a fixed dividend to shareholders, regardless of whether the company pays dividends to owners of common stock. Also, if a company goes bankrupt, owners of preferred stock are in line ahead of common stock owners to receive any proceeds from the company's liquidation. However, preferred stock does not usually give owners a voting say in corporate matters, and common stock does.

Bonds

Owning stock means an investor owns a share of a company, and owning bonds means an investor is lending money to a company or government body.

Bonds, it's said, are basically the IOUs of the business world. When a company or government body wants to raise cash (usually to finance operations or specific projects), it can issue bonds to investors. They are likened to IOUs because each bond states the amount of the loan (the "face value"), the annual interest rate the borrower will pay to the bond owner (the "coupon"), and the date of the scheduled loan repayment ("the maturity"). The amount of time scheduled to pass between when a bond is issued when the loan is repaid (or "redeemed") is referred to as the "term."

If you bought a new $10,000, 20-year bond paying 6 percent interest and then held that bond to maturity, you could usually expect to receive annual interest payments of $600 over the course of that period. After 20 years, the bond issuer would repay the amount of the original loan (the $10,000). Under those neat-and-tidy circumstances, the bond's annual "yield" to the investor would be 6 percent—the stated interest rate. The bonds "total return" would also be 6 percent.

However, things aren't always that simple in the real world. You see, bond investors don't always buy bonds on the day of issue and hold them to maturity. Quite often (especially in the world of professional investors, such as mutual fund managers), people buy and resell bonds before maturity on the so-called "secondary market." And depending on interest rate trends and other factors (such as the financial health of the bond's issuer), investors often buy and sell bonds at prices other than the face value. This makes calculating a bond's yield and total return more complex than simply looking at the stated interest rate.

For example, assume a 10-year, $10,000 bond was issued two years ago with a 6 percent interest rate. Let's also assume that since then, interest rates have risen throughout the economy. As a result, let's say that a newer $10,000, 10-year bond issued by the same issuer now carries a correspondingly higher interest rate, of 7 percent. Because investors on the secondary market know they can receive a 7 percent interest payment from the newer bonds, they'll be much less likely to pay full price for a comparable bond paying a lower interest rate (6 percent). The owner of that lower-rate bond would then probably need to offer the bond at less than face value ("at a discount") in order to attract buyers. Consequently, the original owner of the older bond would lose money if he or she decided to sell at a discount before maturity.

If the original owner did sell at a discount before maturity, then the new owner, who bought the bond at less than face value, would earn a yield greater than the bond's coupon rate. On the secondary bond market, yield no longer depends only upon the coupon rate, but also on the new owner's buying price. Remember: The interest payments are still based on the $10,000 face value, even though the new owner paid less than $10,000 to buy it. For example, if you paid half price ($5,000) for a $10,000 bond with a 6 percent interest rate, then the annual yield on your investment would be double that, or 12 percent. Why? Because the $10,000 bond's 6 percent interest payment amounts to $600, which is 12 percent of the $5,000 you invested. On the secondary market, a bond's total return comes into consideration only when you sell. It takes into account the bond's yield as well as the bond's price change (your profit or loss on the sale).

Don't worry if all this seems confusing. You're not alone. Just keep in mind that the market value (as opposed to the face value) of a bond investment is likely to change if the bond is sold before maturity.

Despite these risks, bond ownership is still generally considered less risky than stock ownership. (Again, though, there are exceptions to most of these general rules. For example, owning a long-term junk bond may be a lot riskier than owning the stock of a well-established, financially sound company.) All of which goes to show that investments can be fairly easy to describe in broad, sweeping terms, but also that the various nuances and variables inherent in the investment markets can make the realities of buying, selling, and owning investments quite complex.

Now back to bond basics.

Just as any two stock investments are different, so too are any two bond investments. For the most part, bond issuers are described based on two characteristics—the type of organizations they are, and their perceived "creditworthiness." (Evaluating creditworthiness is a way of considering how likely an issuer may be to default on interest and redemption payments.) As with consumer debt, the more likely a borrower is to default on a debt, the higher the interest rate the borrower will be required to pay on that debt.

The main categories of bonds are:

➤ Federal government bonds

➤ Government agency bonds

➤ Municipal bonds

➤ Corporate bonds

Federal Government Bonds

The U.S. government borrows money from investors by issuing bonds through the U.S. Treasury Department. Because the federal government is widely considered to be the most creditworthy borrower in the world, Treasury debt usually pays lower interest rates than other bonds with comparable maturities issued by any other issuer.

Federal government debts with maturities of 10 years or more are usually referred to as "Treasury bonds," whereas those with maturities between one and 10 years are called "Treasury notes." Very short-term Treasury debts (maturities of one year or less) are referred to as "Treasury bills," or, more commonly "T-bills."

Because longer-term loans are usually considered riskier than shorter-term loans (regardless of the issuer), Treasury bonds usually pay higher interest rates than Treasury notes, which usually pay higher interest rates than T-bills. Within recent years, the U.S. government has also begun to issue inflation-indexed bonds that attempt to protect bond investors from the risk associated with rising interest rates by automatically increasing the interest rate each time policy makers raise interest rates for borrowers.

Government Agency Bonds

These are issued not by the U.S. Treasury directly, but by specific government-backed agencies, such as the Student Loan Marketing Association (Sallie Mae) and the Federal National Mortgage Association (Fannie Mae). Creditworthiness is determined on a case-by-case basis, and may be influenced by the financial outlook on whatever project the bonds are being used to finance.

Municipal Bonds

Municipal bonds are issued by state and local municipalities (cities, counties, towns, state governments), usually to finance a particular capital project, such as a construction job. If your community has recently built a new school, town hall, or sewage facility, there's a good chance that it issued bonds—municipal bonds—to come up with the money.

Municipal bonds are particularly attractive to investors who want to minimize their investment-related tax burdens. You see, the interest payments from these bonds—unlike the interest income from every other type of bond investment—is tax-free in the eyes of the IRS, and may also be tax-free on your state tax return if you live in the state or local community where the municipal bond was issued.

At first glance "munis" appear to pay lower yields than other, comparable bonds, because they offer lower interest rates. But when you factor in their tax-free status, they actually provide a take-home yield on par with higher-interest, taxable bonds. If you were an investor in the 25 percent federal income tax bracket, you would need to own a taxable bond paying 8 percent interest in order to realize (after taxes) the same return you'd get from a tax-free muni paying just 6 percent. The phrase investors use to describe this comparison is "taxable-equivalent yield." They might say, "For investors in the 25 percent tax bracket, the muni paying 6 percent interest has a taxable-equivalent yield of 8 percent."

Corporate Bonds

As the name implies, these bonds are issued by corporations. And since different companies have different financial characteristics, the risk and return potential of corporate bonds can vary significantly.

Creditworthiness

As mentioned earlier, bonds are also categorized according to their issuers' creditworthiness. But whereas it's relatively easy to identify issuers, it's much more complex to identify their creditworthiness. That's why the responsibility for that job falls to highly trained credit analysts at independent, third-party organizations, such as Standard & Poor's (S&P) and Moody's. Credit analysts take into account a wide variety of information in order to arrive at an understanding of how risky (or safe) each issuer's bonds may be.

A credit analyst's job might include a detailed study of an issuer's business strategy, management, competitors, debt level, cash flow, earnings, and specific market sector. If the issuer is a government body—such as a state government—instead of a company, analysts may look at its tax revenues, budget, regional economy, etc. After doing all of their homework, analysts then assign a letter grade to each issuer, similar to the letter grades school teachers give to their students. The bonds of issuers with good credit quality are referred to as "investment grade." Their issuers are rewarded for their financial well-being by being allowed to offer investors lower interest rates, which means that their costs of doing business are lower.

Investors who don't want much risk in their bond portfolios are happy to receive less interest income in exchange for the relative peace of mind that comes with owning highly rated bonds. Bonds from lower-rated issuers are referred to as "below investment grade," "high yield," or "junk" bonds. Investors who are willing to roll the dice and take bigger risks in exchange for bigger interest payments are likely to be drawn to these types of bonds. Table 4–1 illustrates the basics of Standard & Poor's bond rating systems.

Keep in mind, though, that there's no guarantee an issuer's credit rating will remain unchanged. If a previously well-respected issuer

TABLE 4-1. Standard & Poor's Bond Ratings

Standard & Poor's Bond Issuer Ratings

AAA—Extremely strong financial security characteristics

AA—Very strong financial security characteristics

A—Strong financial security characteristics

BBB—Good financial security characteristics

BB—Marginal financial security characteristics

B—Weak financial security characteristics

CCC—Very weak financial security characteristics

CC—Extremely weak financial security characteristics

NR—Not rated

experiences a financial turn for the worse, credit analysts could "downgrade" the issuer's bonds by replacing its rating with a lower one. Or, if an issuer's financial situation improves, analysts could "upgrade" the rating by assigning a higher rating. This happens on a regular basis, to issuers both large and small. For example, the economic downturn that weakened the U.S. economy in the early years of the twenty-first century also helped to weaken the economies of several states, which were subsequently downgraded. The governments of those states can still issue new bonds, but the bonds must pay a higher rate of interest than would have been the case before the downgrades.

If you think this type of "high finance" doesn't matter to people like us, think again. As taxpayers, we're the ones who are often on the hook for coming up with that extra money. If you live in a community or state that has been downgraded, you might have to pay higher taxes to enable the government to pay higher interest rates to its lenders, or you might lose public services that the government decides it can no longer afford to provide. No matter how you slice it, though, a downgrade of your state or local government's credit rating could affect your wallet in noticeable ways.

There's one more thing you might notice about the bond market, and that's the fact that yields of existing bonds on the secondary market (and the planned interest rates on future bonds) often rise in response to ostensibly good news about the direction in which the economy appears to be headed. In this context, good news refers to things like low unemployment, an increase in the number of factory orders nationwide, and reports predicting strong economic growth. That's because a "hot" economy, for a variety of reasons, increases the likelihood of inflation, and by extension, of future interest rate hikes by the Federal Reserve. (The "Fed" oversees the nation's banking industry.) A sluggish economy, on the other hand, is usually associated with lower interest rates and a diminished chance of inflation.

If interest rates rise, that means new bonds issued after the rate increase will probably pay correspondingly higher interest rates than comparable bonds issued before the rate hike. That, in turn, would lower the resale value of those older bonds. So if you turn on the evening news and hear good things about the nation's economy, there's a good chance that bond prices may have fallen (or might fall) on the secondary market.

Even if that "good" news hasn't yet prompted the Federal Reserve's policymakers to actually raise rates, the very suggestion that it might happen could be enough to cause worried investors to devalue the bonds that are currently being bought and sold on the secondary market. Also, if investors are convinced that the Fed is likely to raise rates in the near future, bond issuers may be forced to offer higher interest rates (yields) on the new bonds they're getting ready to issue, even though the Fed may not have acted yet.

Money Market and Cash Investments

These are conservative, short-term fixed-income securities, and may include "cash equivalents" (such as T-bills) as well as debt contracts between large financial institutions. There's more to it than that if you're interested, but for the purposes of this book's general overview, that's basically what you need to know.

So how do these options stack up against each other when it comes to investment returns? Simply put, stocks have always provided the highest long-term average returns, followed by bonds and money market investments, respectively.

For the 10-year period from 1994 to 2003, stock market total returns (which include reinvested dividends) rose an average of 13.04 percent annually, bond returns increased an average of 7.53 percent, and cash equivalents increased 4.15 percent.

Over longer periods, the results have been similar. During the 20-year period from 1984 to 2003, stocks rose 14.29 percent, followed by bonds at 11.21 percent and cash at 5.22 percent. Going back through the 50-year period that began in 1954, stocks came out on top (13.07 percent), followed by bonds (6.86 percent) and money markets (5.31 percent).

FYI: An investment's "real return" is its return minus the rate of inflation for the same period. During the past 10 years, the average inflation rate was 2.37 percent. It averaged 3.04 percent during the past 20 years, and 3.97 percent during the past half century.

A High Priority:
Understanding Asset Allocation

Professional investors have their own special lingo to describe the products, theories, and strategies they use to help themselves (and clients) pursue financial goals. Whereas you and I might be inclined to say, "I picked a mix of different investments to own in my account," a professional investor might say, "I selected the specific securities to include in my portfolio's asset allocation." We already mentioned that "portfolio" is just a fancy way of saying "investment account." Now you know that "asset allocation" simply means "investment mix."

If half of your investments were stocks and the other half were bonds, you might say, "My portfolio's asset allocation is 50 percent stocks and 50 percent bonds." A riskier allocation would typically include more stocks (such as 75 percent stocks and 25 percent bonds), and a more conservative allocation would include more bonds and/or cash investments and fewer stocks.

The reason the concept of asset allocation is so important is that the specific mix of investments you select will be one of the key factors influencing your portfolio's current level of risk as well as its potential for future growth.

Many investors and analysts even go so far as to say that the overall asset allocation you select is more important to your future returns than the specific investments you own within that asset allocation. In other words, the fact that you have a portfolio of 50 percent stocks and 50 percent bonds may be more of a "determinant" of your future investment success than the fact that you chose to invest half of your money in the stocks of X, Y, and Z companies and half of your money in the bonds of issuers A, B, and C.

An influential study published several years ago backed up this theory with cold, hard data. According to its authors, asset allocation was responsible for more than 93 percent of variation in portfolio performance. It's not necessary to read the entire study in order to appreciate the significance of your asset allocation decisions, but at least now you'll know why some people believe it's so important to think about your overall asset allocation first and your actual investment choices second.

Of course, there are undoubtedly some very successful investors who disagree with those findings. Many talented and lucky investors alike have made hefty profits by buying the "right" investments at low prices and selling them at high prices. But ignoring big-picture asset allocation decisions in order to roll the dice on individual stocks or bonds can be a risky proposition, and it's probably not the strategy most people should rely on as they attempt to invest their way to a more financially secure future. (We'll get to the risk-reducing benefits of diversification momentarily.)

Rebalance? Why and How

You should also understand that your portfolio's asset allocation is always subject to change, due to the fact that investment performance could cause the value of some assets to rise (or fall) more dramatically than others. For example, let's assume again that you have a portfolio of 50 percent stocks and 50 percent bonds. If the value of your stock investments were to grow faster than the value of the bonds, you would no longer have a 50/50 mix. You could end up with

55 percent stocks and 45 percent bonds, or 81 and 19 percent, or some other mix. On the other hand, if your stock investments lost value, the opposite could occur. You might end up with 35 percent stocks and 65 percent bonds, or whatever.

When a portfolio changes like that, people say it has "shifted" or become "unbalanced." As a result, you might need to "rebalance" in order to regain your portfolio's original risk and return potential. If a 50/50 portfolio shifted so that you suddenly owned 55 percent stocks and 45 percent bonds, you could opt either to keep that new allocation or rebalance back to the 50/50 mix. One way to rebalance would be to sell some of your stocks and reinvest the proceeds in bonds until you have a 50/50 mix again. Or you could keep all of your stocks, but add new money to your bond allocation (that is, buy more bonds), until the value of your bond allocation matches the value of your stock allocation.

Experts typically suggest that you rebalance at least once, perhaps twice, each year. Since it's a good idea to meet with your investment advisor annually, you should make it a priority to talk about rebalancing during that meeting.

Also, just as no two stock or bond investments have identical risk and performance potential, you can't assume that two comparable asset allocations have identical performance characteristics. For example, Paul and Richard might each have a portfolio of 50 percent stocks and 50 percent bonds, but that doesn't mean they'll earn the same returns or encounter the same risks. If Paul invests exclusively in small-cap stocks and junk bonds, and Richard invests only in well-established stocks and AAA-rated bonds, then Richard would in all likelihood have a less risky portfolio. Paul could potentially earn higher returns in the long run, but he might also suffer bigger losses too. There's no way of knowing for sure.

Don't Put All Your Eggs in One Basket—Diversify!

A few paragraphs back you read that ignoring asset allocation in order to roll the dice on individual investments can be a risky proposition, and that it's probably not the strategy most people should rely on as they attempt to invest their way to a more financially secure future. That's because putting all of your investment dollars into just one or two individual investments could be the financial equivalent of putting all of your eggs in one basket. If something bad happens to your basket (or your investment), then you could lose all of your eggs (or money).

For most people, a better strategy is to "diversify" a portfolio by putting money into a mix of different and potentially complementary investments (i.e., putting eggs into different baskets). That way, if one investment loses value, other investments might simultaneously grow in value and offset the loss.

If you only invest in one stock, for example, and its share price falls by 40 percent, then your entire stock portfolio would lose 40 percent of its value. But if you invest in several different stocks, and the share price of one stock falls by 40 percent while the price of another rises 100 percent and the price of a third stays the same, you could still break even or perhaps come out ahead (depending on how much of your money is invested in each stock). As this example shows, diversification is a potentially powerful strategy for reducing risk and, by extension, increasing a portfolio's value.

These oft-repeated observations certainly shouldn't obscure the fact that some investors have grown quite rich by ignoring diversification. Maybe you've heard someone talk about the family friend (or coworker, neighbor, etc.) who invested almost exclusively in one company's stock, dating back to the days when most people had never heard of the now famous company. The risk paid off, the story usually goes, and that nondiversified investor eventually owned a single-stock portfolio worth millions of dollars.

Not bad. But for every success story like that, you could easily find another about someone who risked it all on one company and ended up with a bunch of worthless stock. (Just think of all the "paper millionaires" in the 1990s who owned stock in companies that went from boom to bust almost overnight. Lots of people in that position were worth big bucks on paper, but when their stock prices plummeted, so did their net worth.)

What's the Difference?

It's not uncommon for people who are new to investing to get confused about the difference between asset allocation and diversification. After all, each concept relates to the mix of investments you own. But do you remember the difference between strategy (big-picture goals) and tactics (the actual techniques used to achieve a specific objective)? When it comes to investing, asset allocation refers to your overall strategy, such as investing half of your money in stocks and half in bonds. Diversification refers to the actual investment selection tactics you use within your asset allocation, such as choosing several different stock and bond investments that have the potential to consistently increase the value of your portfolio over time.

Think of it this way: Everyone who invests has an asset allocation. But not everyone is diversified. For example, if Randy owns only one company's stock, then he has a 100 percent stock asset allocation. But his portfolio is not diversified. On the other hand, if Jeff owns the stocks of 10 different companies with different business characteristics, he also has a 100 percent stock asset allocation, but unlike Randy, Jeff's portfolio is diversified. If one of Jeff's 10 stocks happens to be the same stock Randy owns, Jeff would be exposed to much less risk if that company experiences tough times.

But owning more than one stock (or bond) investment doesn't automatically mean that you have a well-diversified portfolio. If you own stock in 10 different companies that only make ball bearings for tractor factories, for instance, then you're probably not very well diversified. If the tractor industry suddenly goes belly-up, you'll probably be out of luck pretty quickly.

When you get right down to it, investing can have a lot in common with gambling if you don't take steps to manage the risks involved. (Of course, you probably won't find many gambling analogies in the educational literature provided by investment firms.) Diversification, therefore, can be seen as a strategy that prevents investors from placing all of their chips on one bet.

CHAPTER 5

Mutual Fund Know-How

For the most part, everything we have discussed so far has applied to individual "securities"—individual stocks and bonds. However, millions of Americans participate in the stock and bond markets without ever directly buying an actual stock or bond. How? By investing in mutual funds.

A mutual fund is essentially a big investment account run by a professional investment manager (or a team of managers) in the interests of individual investors who purchase shares of the fund. The value of your investment in a fund is determined by the investment performance of the securities owned by the fund. When an investor buys shares of a small-cap fund, for instance, he or she turns money over to the fund manager, who combines it with the money contributed by other people and then invests it in the stocks of different small-cap companies. The fund's share price rises or falls depending on whether the overall value of the small-cap stock investments selected by management rises or falls.

Technically speaking, a mutual fund is an "investment company." When you buy fund shares, you're purchasing shares of ownership in the fund. The Investment Company Institute is the nonprofit organization that monitors and advocates on behalf of the U.S. mutual fund industry. To learn more about important trends and current events in the mutual fund industry, visit its Web site, at www.ici.org.

Usually, the risk/return potential of a specific fund is comparable to that of the assets in which it invests. Large-cap stock funds can typically be expected to have the same general characteristics as large-cap companies, small-cap stock funds will have the character-istics of small-cap companies, and so on. But there's a big difference between investing in individual securities on your own and investing in a mutual fund that owns the same type of investments, and it can be summed up in one important word: diversification.

Although the strategy of diversification sounds fairly simple when you talk about not putting all of your eggs in one basket, as we touched upon in the last chapter, properly diversifying a portfolio on your own is actually easier said than done. To make consistently well-informed decisions about what to own in a diversified portfo-lio, you either need to have significant professional training and experience or lots of time on your hands to identify, sift through, and interpret all of the meaningful data and analysis that's available on individual stocks and bonds. No matter how smart or enthusiastic you are, that's a tall order. By investing in mutual funds, however, you turn those responsibilities over to someone who has all of those attributes and resources—the fund manager.

It's the fund manager's job to try to accomplish the fund's stated objective. Someone who manages an "Equity Income" fund, for example, has the responsibility of investing in the stock of compa-nies (equities) that pay dividends (income). Therefore, the manager would focus his or her research and investment strategies on divi-dend-paying companies. If the manager happens to uncover infor-mation about several intriguing companies that don't pay dividends, then he probably won't invest in them, for the simple reason that they don't pay dividends. (It's worth noting, though, that fund managers often have the option of investing some of their fund's money in assets other than those that meet the fund's primary investment objective. The upcoming discussion on prospectuses will explain how you can find out exactly what type of assets a particular fund's manager is allowed to purchase.)

You might not think so at first, but some fund managers have very interesting jobs. For example, the manager of a so-called "leisure fund," which invests primarily in companies that cater to people's desire for fun and relaxation, may spend time on the road, browsing through toy stores, visiting casinos, and trying out new games at video game conventions. With his fund's potential investments in mind, he might ask for help buying a present for child, with questions like, "What video games are popular with kids these days?" and, "Which brand of stuffed animals is particularly popular?" He might also visit hotels and casinos, making quiet observations about customer service, popular attractions, and even which establishments offer the best perks to their regular customers.

If you were to notice this man in a toy aisle, video game trade show, or hotel casino, you might just assume he's a father shopping for a present, a gambler on vacation, or maybe just a traveling businessman with nothing more on his mind than finding ways to kill some time. But in reality he's working at making his mutual fund more profitable for its investors. The insights he gains by leaving the office and thinking like a leisure-minded consumer help him determine which companies are doing things right and which ones aren't. After carefully assessing the data he and his financial analysts have gathered, as well as the lessons he's learned from cashiers, front desk clerks, and teenage gamers, he decides which stocks to buy and sell in order to earn the best possible returns for the fund's investors.

Fund managers have all kinds of interesting insights that might help fatten the wallets of their fund's investors. On one occasion, I interviewed a fund manager who researched and invested in various retail establishments. When he mentioned that he liked the company that owns a chain of grocery stores where I often shopped, I asked him why. He spoke in detail about the company's management philosophy. He said he liked that the company owns rather than rents much of its real estate, and also that the company buys many of its products directly from manufacturers, thereby reducing the costs of dealing with a middleman. It was an interesting conversation.

Being a fund manager isn't all shopping, fun, and games, of course. The manager of a utilities fund, for example, must be intimately familiar with every factor that could influence the share prices of the companies in which the fund invests. That might mean understanding the significance of ongoing labor negotiations, new federal regulations, emerging competition, and corporate management practices. On Monday, the manager might spend several hours reading reports and analysis about a power plant he'll be visiting on Tuesday. On Tuesday, he might spend the morning touring the power plant and the afternoon interviewing the company's managers for insights as to whether to invest.

And again, even if a manager likes a company, he or she will still need to decide if owning it would help the fund achieve its objectives. If one of these stated objectives is to maintain a diversified asset allocation, then the manager would need to determine whether the company in question is too similar to the other companies already owned by the fund. If it is, the next decision might be about which company to own and which one to leave behind. It's a lot of work, and most of us just don't have the time or the training to do it right.

Not all funds are "actively" managed in such a manner, though. Some funds are "passively" managed, which means they own a predetermined mix of investments that rarely changes. Most passively managed funds own the same investments as a specific market "index" or "benchmark," and they change that mix only when the index makes a change.

An index is a statistical model that tracks the cumulative performance of a group of different investments. For example, the Dow Jones Industrial Average and the Standard & Poor's Composite Index of 500 Stocks (S&P 500) are indexes based on the cumulative stock prices of two different groups of companies. On any given day, the value of each index will rise or fall depending on whether most of the stocks in the index rose or fell in value. This isn't a perfect analogy, but you could compare an index to a baseball team's batting average. On any given day, some players will hit the ball better than others. Depending on whether more players improve their individual average or lower it with their performance at the plate that day, the team's overall batting average will rise or fall.

However, whether you choose actively managed funds or passively managed funds, investing in mutual funds doesn't relieve you of the need to diversify. You need a diversified mix of funds—or a single fund that attempts to consistently offer a "targeted" level of diversification, designed to meet the unique needs of a specific type of investor.

Also, keep in mind that there is a price to pay for investing in mutual funds—literally. Unlike individual stock and bond investments, mutual funds require investors to pay various fees and expenses, some of which you may find easier to swallow than others. Most funds charge a management fee, for instance, in order to help compensate the managers who run the fund. Since actively managed funds typically require much more work than passively managed funds, their fees are usually higher. You'd probably agree that it's fair to charge investors for the privilege of having a financial professional make well-informed investment decisions for them, but you might be surprised to learn how much money some of these folks rake in each year!

On the other hand, you might not be quite so happy to pay for the fund's marketing expenses. Yet that's exactly what many funds make their investors do. The so-called 12(b)1 fee charged by many funds is earmarked specifically for marketing expenses. So if you ever see a full-page ad for one of your funds in the pages of a glossy national magazine, check to see if you're paying a 12(b)1 fee. If you are, then part of your investment returns never made it into your pocket. Instead, the money may have been used to hire an ad agency and then to pay for the placement of that ad.

Of course, you may be required to pay brokerage fees to buy individual securities. But the investments themselves don't charge the same type of additional expenses as mutual funds.

Read the Prospectus Before Investing

Maybe you've met one of these people at the water cooler (possibly during the stock market boom of the late 1990s), or maybe you've only seen them in the movies. They love to talk about investing, and they always seem to have a hot tip on the next big thing. They might even be the nicest, most trustworthy people you know. But that's no excuse for you to impulsively invest in the who-knows-what-it-might-be company or fund they're talking about. Before you ever invest money in a publicly traded company or fund, you should familiarize yourself with that particular investment's prospectus.

A prospectus is a legal document produced by the issuer of an investment—such as a company or a mutual fund—that describes in detail all of the general information necessary for an investor to begin making a well-informed decision. Someone who is thinking about investing directly in the stock of an individual company "listed" on the stock market should obtain and read that company's prospectus before doing so. And someone who is thinking about investing in a specific fund should make a point of reading that fund's prospectus. Better yet, they should read and compare the prospectuses of several other investments too, in order to make an even more well-informed decision.

Because a lot of people reading this book are probably more likely to invest in funds (through retirement plans, for example), let's start out with an overview of a typical mutual fund prospectus. The format and legal requirements for all prospectuses are largely the same. Most prospectuses will include:

➤ **Introduction.** This brief opening statement identifies the exact name of the mutual fund and its primary investment objectives. It summarizes the information you will read in the pages that follow, and may explain specific features of the prospectus—that the prospectus, for instance, specifically identifies the type of investor who should consider investing in the fund. If the fund has a particularly noteworthy risk consideration, the introduction may also make that clear; for example, if a fund's investments are concentrated primarily on one specific business sector or only in high-risk, small-company stocks. The prospectus may also point out the potential pros and cons of investing in the fund, as well as alternatives.

➤ **Objective**. This is a brief (one- or two-sentence) description of the fund's investment strategy.

➤ **Principal investment strategies.** This is a more detailed description of the fund's asset allocation strategy. It states whether the fund allocates its assets among stocks, bonds, and cash, and provides general parameters to indicate what the fund's typical asset allocation would be. If the fund typically invests up to 50 percent of its assets in U.S. stocks, up to 25 percent in foreign stocks, and up to 25 percent in bonds, you'll see it in print here. Other investment strategies described here might include the fact that a fund evaluates bond investments by placing more emphasis on the outlook for economic growth and interest rates, instead of on the credit ratings of the issuers. Also, you can learn here whether the fund invests in the United States exclusively, or in foreign securities as well.

➤ **Principal risks.** All investments carry some element of risk, and this section of the prospectus gives you a general idea of the potential risks you could face by investing in the fund. For example, for a fund that can own foreign investments, the prospectus would contain language informing you that these investments carry unique risks beyond those you might encounter with an American investment; risks related to currency fluctuations, government regulation, negative political or legal developments, differences in financial record keeping, and less strict oversight of foreign markets.

➤ **Who should consider investing in the fund?** This section addresses the question of which type of investor the fund may be appropriate for. Depending on the particular prospectus, it might be a fairly straightforward overview of suitable investors, such as: "Investors seeking capital appreciation who are willing to accept the risks of investing in a fund that invests primarily in growth-oriented common stocks of small-cap companies." It might also declare whether the fund may be an appropriate "core" holding for investors who do not want to worry much about diversifying their own portfolios.

➤ **Performance information.** The data here illustrates the fund's annual returns during a specified period of time, such as the previous 10 years or since the fund's "inception" (creation). It also compares those returns with the performance of a relevant market index during the same period. If a fund has more than one "class" of share, such as Class A shares and Class B shares, it will show the returns of each. (The main difference between various class shares of the same fund is usually the expenses charged by each to investors.)

> **Fees and expenses.** The exact value of the maximum shareholder fees charged by each class of fund shares is expressed here as a percentage of the share price.

> **Annual operating expenses.** This will tell you what percentage of share assets is devoted to management fees, 12b-1 fees, annual operating expenses, and other costs.

> **Fund in detail.** Some prospectuses may also contain an additional page spelling out in even greater detail how the fund defines certain types of investments. Other information here tells you the type of research that fund management relies on to select investments for the fund, when the fund might sell investments, and under what circumstances the fund might veer from its stated investment objectives.

The prospectus of an individual company, on the other hand, includes information only on that company and its securities, including any risks they may present to investors. Because investors purchase individual securities outside of mutual fund accounts, there is nothing comparable to the information in a fund prospectus about management fees, fund operating expenses, etc.

You can also learn a lot about a specific company by reading its annual report. Like a prospectus, an annual report is a document that companies must file each year, as required by the Securities and Exchange Commission (SEC), which governs the nation's investment markets.

As you may have expected, though, there's more to successful investing than simply choosing the right mix of mutual funds or individual securities. The topics covered in the following chapter—monitoring your portfolio's performance, understanding its risk, paying taxes on earnings, and working with a professional—are all important priorities too.

CHAPTER 6

Real World Investment Tips

In the last chapter, during the discussion of passively managed mutual funds, we referred to stock market indexes, also known as benchmarks. To refresh your memory, an index is not a physical thing, but rather, a statistical representation of the overall performance of a specific group of investments.

The two indexes previously mentioned—the S&P 500 and the Dow Jones Industrial Average—are two of the most closely watched in the world. The S&P 500 tracks the prices of 500 of the largest American companies. "The Dow" also follows large companies, but tracks only those stocks issued by 30 of the market's most influential and highly regarded companies. Such stocks are often called "blue chips," in reference to the most expensive poker chips a gambler can buy. Therefore, the Dow is often called the stock market's blue chip index. There are scores of other indexes out there too. Some follow stocks in various market sectors, countries, and regions. You can also find more narrowly focused benchmarks.

Market benchmarks are useful—make that indispensable—for two main reasons: They can help investors better understand potential investments, and they can help investors gauge the relative performance of the investments they already own.

For example, an investor who's considering a certain type of investment—such as buying shares in a Latin American stock fund— can research that investment by studying the performance and characteristics of indexes that monitor the Latin American market. He or she might then narrow down the list of potential fund investments by eliminating those that have "underperformed" the major benchmarks for that market in the past.

And investors who own a particular investment—such as Latin American stock fund shares—can use benchmarks to determine whether their particular investment is performing up to par with similar investments, by comparing their investment's ongoing returns to the returns of the relevant benchmark. (Remember, a fund's prospectus will tell you which index serves as the fund's benchmark.)

Standard & Poor's is generally considered to be a worldwide leader in investment market monitoring and reporting, including the creation and publication of a wide variety of indexes. Other leading companies offering index services are Dow Jones, Morgan Stanley Capital International (MSCI), and the Frank Russell Company, to name but a few. Here are brief descriptions of 12 Standard & Poor's indexes:

> **S&P Global 1200.** Covers 1,200 companies in 29 countries in seven geographical regions around the world.

> **S&P 500.** Generally considered representative of the U.S. stock market, this index tracks the prices of 500 top large-cap companies in leading industries throughout the U.S. economy.

> **S&P SmallCap 600.** The 600 small companies in this index represent about 3 percent of the U.S. stock market.

> **S&P MidCap 400.** The 400 midsized companies in this index account for about 7 percent of the U.S. market.

> **S&P Europe 350.** Covers approximately 70 percent of Europe's market cap spanning 17 different stock markets.

> **S&P/TOPIX 150.** Tracks the prices of stocks from each major sector of the Tokyo market.

> **S&P/TSX 60.** Monitors 60 large Canadian companies from 10 different economic sectors

➤ **S&P/ASX 50.** If you're looking for insights into the stock performance of the 50 largest companies in the Australian market, then turn your attention here.

➤ **S&P Asia 50.** Tracks stock prices in Hong Kong, Korea, Taiwan, and Singapore, and represents about 70 percent of each country's market cap.

➤ **S&P Latin America 40.** Companies from Mexico, Brazil, Argentina, and Chile are represented in this index, which accounts for about 70 percent of each country's market cap.

➤ **S&P 700.** This index is essentially the S&P Global 1200 minus the S&P 500. It consists of all the stocks in the S&P Europe 350, S&P/TOPIX 150, S&P/ASX 50, S&P/TSX 60, S&P Asia 50, and S&P Latin America 40.

➤ **S&P Global 100.** The collective performance of 100 multinational companies accounts for the performance of this index.

As noted earlier, Standard & Poor's does not have a monopoly on the index business. For example, other notable indexes include:

➤ **MSCI's Europe, Australasia, Far East (EAFE) Index.** The EAFE is a frequently cited indicator of stock price movements in 21 developed markets around the world.

➤ **Nikkei Index and Heng Seng Index.** These are indexes for the Tokyo and Hong Kong stock exchanges, respectively.

➤ **Russell 2000 Index.** The Russell 2000, which tracks 2,000 small companies' stock prices, is an oft-cited barometer of the small-cap market.

➤ **Nasdaq Composite Index.** The "Nasdaq" covers more than 5,000 stocks traded on the Nasdaq market, and is frequently looked upon as a reflection of high-tech sector performance.

➤ **Lehman Brothers Aggregate Bond Index.** This index attempts to shed light on bond investments in general by incorporating data from several other bond indexes in order to depict overall bond market performance.

Your Goals, Time Frame, and Risk Tolerance

Understanding the different characteristics and return potential of the three main asset classes in general—and of specific investments in particular—is an important aspect of any investor's job. An additional requirement for building a portfolio that will effectively serve your needs is to understand what makes you tick, in a financial sense. What are you trying to accomplish by investing? When would you like to accomplish those goals? And how much risk can you tolerate on a day-to-day, month-to-month, and year-to-year basis while you're investing to achieve those goals?

Defining your goals is the first challenge. If you know that you'll need a certain amount of money in order to afford a specific product, service, or lifestyle, then you essentially know what your goal is. The key phrase is "know that you'll need a certain amount of money." Saying that you've got a goal without knowing how much it will cost doesn't really get you where you need to be. Do you want the success of your top priorities to be dependent on random guesswork or blind optimism? Probably not. It's one thing to say that you're investing for retirement. It's another thing altogether to know how much money you'll need to accumulate in order to retire and enjoy the lifestyle you've been looking forward to.

Regardless of your particular goal, you should make every effort to arrive at a well-informed decision based on a rational assessment of two facts: how much it would cost to finance the goal in today's dollars, and how much more that goal will actually cost by the time you hope to achieve it. Sure, there will be some guesswork involved. After all, it's impossible to predict the future. But based on past economic trends and current research into the price of your goal, you should be able to come up with a fairly accurate estimate.

In this case, past economic trends pertain primarily to inflation. Since the end of World War Two, overall prices in the U.S. economy have risen in all but two years. With that in mind, you can be reasonably sure that the price of whatever it is you hope to purchase will also rise between now and the time you're ready to spend. But there's a big difference between the low single-digit inflation that's been the norm during the last several years and the staggering double-digit inflation that shocked consumers in the early 1970s.

How do you take those variations into account in your own planning? Start by looking at long-term historical average rates of inflation as an indication of how much prices are likely to rise in the future. For example, if you're trying to identify the future cost of a goal that's 20 years away, you could start by figuring out how much it would cost now. Then, in order to identify its likely future cost, you'd need to perform a calculation based on what you think the average annual rate of inflation will be over the next 20 years. Many people try to arrive at an idea of future inflation rates by looking at historic rates of inflation during comparable time periods in the past. So if you're thinking about the cost of a goal that's 20 years away, it can be informative to look at the average annual inflation rate during the past 20 years.

Taking it a step further, you could also examine what the average rate of inflation had been for all 20-year periods during the past 40 or 50 years or so (from 1955 through 1974, from 1956 through 1975, etc.). After you get a general idea about past trends, you can make an educated guess about future inflation trends.

For example, during the 20-year period comprising 1984 through 2003, the average rate of inflation—as measured by the U.S. Department of Labor's consumer price index (CPI)—was 3.4 percent. But going back to the 1930s, the highest annual inflation rate was 18.13 percent in 1946, and the lowest was –10.27 percent in 1932. (It's worth noting that prices have only fallen in two other years since 1932's decline, the last time in 1954.)

With that in mind, let's assume Jeff wants to be able to maintain his current standard of living when he retires in 20 years. In order to do that, he itemizes his anticipated expenses and determines that he would need to spend the equivalent of $40,000 each year. But that $40,000 is today's price tag, in today's dollars, and Jeff is thinking ahead 20 years. Obviously, prices will have risen by the time Jeff's retirement rolls around. The question for Jeff is: How much more will things cost? How much money will he likely need to spend in 20 years in order to afford a lifestyle that costs $40,000 today?

If Jeff decided to operate under the assumption that the average annual inflation rate during the next 20 years is going to match the 3.02 percent average annual rate of the past 20 years, then he should expect to need $72,807 in future dollars in order to afford today's $40,000 life.

(Needless to say, most people don't plan for a one-year retirement, so the example above does not paint an accurate picture of how to calculate your retirement savings goal. That's covered in the next chapter.)

In some cases, the distant past won't shed nearly as much light on your needs as the recent past, particularly if research reveals that cost trends related to your goal have undergone a dramatic change recently. Within the past few years, for instance, the cost of a college education has been rising at a much higher rate than the overall inflation rate. So relying on long-term average inflation rates wouldn't be particularly helpful when you're calculating the cost of future college education. Instead, you'd be probably be better off basing your estimates on new research into current tuition trends.

Fortunately, you don't need to be a math whiz or an economics guru to quickly and conveniently put a dollars-and-cents price tag on your future financial goals. Regardless what those goals may be, there's almost certainly a free "calculator" program online that will compute the specific data you enter (i.e., current cost of goal, time frame, etc.) and then quickly "crunch the numbers" to identify your savings goal.

Simply identifying your investment time frame should be a much simpler matter, relatively speaking. All you need is to determine exactly what your target date is. Knowing that you want to retire "early" doesn't necessarily nail down your retirement investment time frame. Knowing that you want to retire in exactly 20 years does.

The third factor to consider as part of your investment outlook is your tolerance for risk. As you know, stocks are typically considered the riskiest of the three types of assets, with bonds the second riskiest and cash the least risky. However, higher risk has historically been associated with higher long-term returns. Although stock prices have typically fluctuated most in the short term, they have also risen highest over the long term. Cash has typically had the least price volatility and the lowest returns.

"Aggressive" investors are willing to accept a relatively high degree of risk and typically go for a high allocation of stocks in their portfolio. "Conservative" investors want to minimize risk, and usually scale back on stocks in favor of bonds and cash. "Moderate" investors usually try to seek a balance between the two poles, perhaps by investing in a mix of stocks and more conservative options.

Financial advisors often suggest that investors assume a "risk profile" based on their investment time frame. For example, if Alexandra were investing for a goal that's 20 years away, she might be able to tolerate a stock-heavy portfolio that has high short-term risk potential but also high long-term growth potential. With 20 years to go and the knowledge that stocks have almost always produced the best returns over such time periods, she might not mind the fact that her portfolio's value may rise and fall from day to day or month to month. But if Alexandra were investing for a goal that's only a few years away, she might want to choose a more conservative asset allocation, one focused less on potentially high returns and more on potential price stability.

Measuring Investment Risk

Whenever you create (or review) an investment strategy, your ultimate goal is to choose the "right" investment(s) for your needs. However, there may be times when you've narrowed down a list of potential investments and end up with two or three that share similar investment objectives and historical returns. What do you do then? You do what the pros do—you make a decision based on your assessment of statistical risk analysis. Here's why: Because it's possible that two similar funds with similar return characteristics may actually have very different underlying risk characteristics.

A statistic called "standard deviation" can help you assess an investment's risk potential by measuring how much the investment's value has typically fluctuated above and below its average value. And a stat called "beta" sheds light on how volatile a particular investment has been relative to its overall market by comparing its price swings with the price swings of an appropriate index.

Standard Deviation

For mutual fund investors, standard deviation depicts how much a fund's returns rose or declined during a particular time frame relative to the fund's average return for the same period. The higher a fund's standard deviation, the more its returns have fluctuated, and the riskier the fund may continue to be in the future. Here's how standard deviation works: Assume that two stock funds each have 10 percent average returns during the same time period. Fund A has a standard deviation of 7, which means that its returns have typically been between 3 percent (10 – 7) and 17 percent (10 + 7) during that time. Fund B's standard deviation is 3, meaning that its returns would have only been fluctuating between 7 percent (10 – 7) and 13 percent (10 + 3) most of that time. In other words, Fund A's investors were exposed to more risk than Fund B's investors, but Fund A didn't reward them for that risk by providing higher returns.

Statistically speaking, standard deviation means that a fund's returns could have been expected to fluctuate within the standard deviation range described above approximately 68 percent of the time. Fluctuations twice as significant could have been expected 95 percent of the time. So Fund B (with the 10 percent average return and the standard deviation of 3) would have likely provided returns in the 7 to 13 percent range 68 percent of the time, and returns ranging between 4 and 16 percent 95 percent of the time.

Beta

Whereas standard deviation essentially compares one measure of an investment's performance with another measure of the same investment's performance, beta compares an investment's volatility—its price swings—with that of the broader market.

For mutual funds, the overall market is typically represented by a relevant benchmark, such as the S&P 500. If a fund has a beta of 1.0, that means its performance has moved in tandem with its market benchmark. A beta higher than 1.0 reveals that a fund has been more volatile than its benchmark, and a beta lower than 1.0 indicates less volatility. A beta of 2.0 would indicate that a fund has tended to be twice as volatile as its benchmark—performing 100 percent better in "up" markets and doing 100 percent worse in "down" markets. A beta of 1.1 would indicate that a fund typically performed 10 percent better or worse than its benchmark. For example, if its benchmark index were to rise 20 percent, such a fund would likely rise 22 percent.

You may not need to spend much of your life contemplating the finer points of statistical investment analysis, but understanding concepts such as beta and standard deviation can help you become a more financially savvy investor. Just remember that past performance can never guarantee future results, no matter how compelling that past performance may seem.

Putting Short-Term Market Moves in Perspective

As you can see, a specific investment's average return for a given period of time doesn't necessarily tell you much about the risks involved with that investment, because it doesn't illustrate how widely the investment's value actually fluctuated during that period. The same holds true for the performance of different asset classes. For example, stocks have historically posted better average annual returns than bonds, but for the most part, stock prices have also fluctuated more dramatically than bond market prices during that period.

When the overall returns for a particular market rise by at least 20 percent, that market is referred to as a "bull market." (Just think of a bull charging ahead.) When returns fall by at least 20 percent, that's referred to as a "bear market." (Think of a bear hibernating.) Since 1926, there have been nine bears and eight bulls in the stock market, compared with four bears and eight bulls in the bond market.

If you have a relatively long-term investment time frame, try to stay level-headed about any bouts of short-term market volatility you might encounter along the way. Keep in mind that since 1929, the stock market has posted an annual loss only 22 times. The biggest one-year loss was 43.36 percent in 1931, and the biggest one-year gain was 53.81 percent in 1933. Despite those short-term ups and downs, the long-term value of stocks has continued to grow steadily.

And keep in mind that it's often considered a better idea to pursue a "buy-and-hold" stock investment strategy for long-term goals than to try to "time" the market by frequently buying and selling investment shares. Simply put, "timing" the market could cause you to miss out on some of the market's best growth spurts.

Regardless of the news coming from the markets on any given day, always try to maintain your investment discipline. If you've adequately diversified your portfolio with a complementary mix of investments that addresses your goals and time frame, then you shouldn't lose too much sleep over day-to-day developments.

Dollar Cost Averaging

The investment strategy known as "dollar cost averaging" is basically the exact opposite of timing the market. Despite its sophisticated-sounding name, dollar cost averaging is actually quite simple. All it involves is investing the same amount of money in a particular portfolio on a regular basis, such as once or twice each month. You may even be practicing dollar cost averaging right now without even realizing it. If you automatically contribute a predetermined amount of your income to an employer-sponsored retirement plan investment account every payday, you're dollar cost averaging.

Dollar cost averaging helps you build good savings habits, but that's not all it can do. Because your fixed contribution purchases more shares when prices fall and fewer shares when prices rise, your average *cost* per share could end up being lower than the investment's average *price* per share over time.

For example, assume you invest $100 each month for three months. The first month the share price is $10, so you purchase 10 shares. The second month the share price is down to $5, so you purchase 20 shares. By the third month, the price has risen to $20, so you purchase just five shares. After three months you have spent $300 to own 35 shares, which means that your average cost per share was $8.57 ($300 ÷ 35 shares = $8.57). Yet the average price per share during that three-month period was $11.66 ($10 + $5 + $20 ÷ 3 = $11.66).

In addition to the good habits and investment efficiency it fosters, dollar cost averaging takes some of the guesswork out of investing because it relieves you of the responsibility of trying to choose the best time to buy shares. Not only is dollar cost averaging potentially less risky than timing the market, but you'll probably find it a lot less stressful too.

Before You Sell, Check the Calendar

The reason most people invest is to earn a profit by selling an asset after its value has appreciated. When you sell an investment for more than you paid, that profit is generally referred to as "capital gain." But there's more than one type of capital gain, and ignoring that fact could cost you.

When you sell an investment for profit after owning it less than 12 months, the IRS considers that profit to be a "short-term capital gain." When you sell an asset for profit after owning it more than 12 months, the IRS considers that profit to be a "long-term capital gain." What's the big deal? Long-term capital gains are taxed at lower rates than short-term capital gains. Short-term capital gains are taxed as ordinary income, and federal income tax rates can go as high as 35 percent. But long-term capital gains are not taxed as ordinary income—the highest possible long-term capital gains tax rate is just 20 percent. Investors in the lowest income tax bracket get an even better deal: Their top capital gains tax rate is only 10 percent. If you purchased investments after the year 2000 and hold onto them for at least five years, your capital gains tax rate is even lower. The top rate for five-year capital gains is 18 percent, whereas low-income tax-payers pay only 8 percent.

That's why it's mandatory to check the calendar before you ever sell a profitable investment. Selling just a day or two early could mean that you'll be required to pay significantly higher taxes. Consider the examples of Donna and Gerry, who are both in the 25 percent federal income tax bracket. Each bought stocks at the same time about one year ago, and their investments have each risen in value by $1,000. Gerry didn't check the calendar, and he sold his stocks exactly 11 months and three weeks after the purchase. As a result, his $1,000 capital gain was worth only $750 to him after accounting for his $250 short-term capital gains tax. Donna, however, checked the calendar. She waited until 12 months and one day had passed since her purchase, and then sold her stocks for a $1,000 profit. Donna ended up with $800 in her pocket (compared with Gerry's $750) because her long-term capital gains tax bill was only $200.

There's a flip side to every coin, of course, and when it comes to selling investments, the flip side of a capital gain is a capital loss. When people see one of their investments lose value, one natural reaction is to want to hold on to the investment until its value rises and it becomes profitable. But there may be times when it makes sense to sell an investment at a loss, because the IRS allows taxpayers to offset capital gains with capital losses. In other words, if you report a $1,000 investment gain in the same year that you report a $1,000 investment loss, then you won't owe taxes on the gain. So if you're thinking about "locking in" gains by selling an investment for a profit, and if you're also "sitting" on a losing investment and hoping that its price recovers, it might make sense to sell them at the same time, or at least in the same calendar year. Just don't forget to first determine whether your profit would be considered a long-term or a short-term gain.

Other Types of Investments

Most of the investment-related discussions contained in these pages have focused on mutual funds and on individual stock, bond, and cash securities. That's because the average American can probably address the vast majority of his or her investment objectives by owning those types of investments. But there are other types of investments on the market, so you need to be aware of those as well.

Exchange-Traded Funds

ETFs, as they are known, are investment funds, similar to mutual funds, that try to replicate the exact performance of a particular index by owning the same exact mix of securities as that benchmark. Unlike mutual fund shares (but like individual stocks), ETF shares trade on the stock market. An investor can quickly and conveniently gain exposure to all of the companies monitored by a particular index by purchasing shares of an ETF modeled on that index.

For example, an S&P 500 ETF would own the same 500 stocks tracked by the S&P 500. By purchasing shares of an S&P 500 ETF, you would own a single investment that should perform exactly like that overall group of 500 companies.

Derivatives

Derivatives, such as "options" and "futures," are potentially complicated and risky investment contracts that derive their value from the value of an underlying security. Because of their complex and potentially high-risk nature, they may not be appropriate for novice investors or for investors with limited financial resources.

Real Estate Investment Trusts

REITs, as they're commonly known, are investment vehicles that own real estate–based assets, such as buildings and property. Investors who hope to profit from owning a diversified mix of real estate without actually going out and investing in different properties on their own can pursue that goal by investing in shares of a REIT instead.

Preparing to Work with an Investment Professional

Although this chapter has covered a lot of ground, it only explains the basic principles of investing. To understand in more detail how specific strategies, rules, or considerations may apply to your real-world life, it's a good idea to work on your portfolio with the assistance of a trained investment professional.

Before you schedule a meeting and initiate this important relationship, though, make sure you understand what type of financial professional you're dealing with, and how he or she expects to be paid. A fee-only advisor, for instance, usually charges a flat rate to review your situation and make recommendations, whereas a commission-based broker earns money each time you make an investment. If you only need advice, it probably makes sense to stick with a fee-only investment advisor or financial planner. But if you plan to purchase securities and want the guidance and assistance of a trained professional each step of the way, there's nothing wrong with paying reasonable commissions.

To prepare for the meeting, identify the "big three": your specific financial goals, your exact time frames, and your general feelings about investment risk. If you want to write it all down to present to the advisor, go ahead. While you're at it, jot down any questions you might want to ask. Also, gather any account statements you have that detail current investments, and bring them along too.

No two advisors work exactly alike, but most try to gain an in-depth understanding of each client's needs in order to present ideas for a strategy that addresses those needs. Usually, that boils down to determining the right asset allocation for each client's risk/return objectives, and then selecting the specific investments that will go into the portfolio. After a client's investment strategy is in place, an advisor can provide ongoing performance monitoring of the portfolio and conduct periodic reviews with the client. (Advisors may also try to keep clients focused on long-term goals, instead of allowing them to be sidetracked by short-term events.)

To begin the meeting, an investment advisor will probably ask specific questions about where you stand financially, where you hope to stand eventually, and how you plan to make it all happen. If you're a returning client, the advisor may want to know whether you've experienced any life-changing events since the last meeting, such as a marriage, divorce, or the birth of a child. He or she will probably also ask you to confirm that the goals and time frames you identified in the past still accurately represent your outlook.

Even if you don't schedule the meeting with the intention of discussing your plans for retirement, there's a good chance the advisor will raise the topic. Paying for retirement is likely to be the biggest financial challenge many people will ever face, so saving and investing is probably the most realistic strategy for accumulating enough money to afford it. In general, if an advisor suggests that you begin to invest for a goal that you haven't yet considered, give it some thought. Don't feel obliged to make an on-the-spot decision, but also don't assume that he or she is just trying to get more money from you. The advisor may have simply identified an important area of your financial life that you yourself had previously overlooked.

CHAPTER 7

Retirement Realities

B y the end of the twentieth century, the idea of retirement as our parents or grandparents knew it had essentially disappeared. Gone are the old notions of spending your career in the same job, receiving a pocket watch at your retirement party, and then retiring to a life of leisure paid for by a guaranteed pension and Social Security checks. Instead, the "new retirement" of the twenty-first century is much more uncertain. It requires you to assume a far greater degree of responsibility for your own financial security, due in part to worries about Social Security's future and the way many companies have restructured their retirement benefits packages in recent years.

Until the later twentieth century, most companies that provided retirement benefits to their workers offered so-called "defined benefit" pension plans. DB plans require little work on the part of employees, because the money earmarked for future benefits payments is set aside by the company and managed by a team of financial experts and investment advisors. When a worker retires, the company begins making the promised retirement income payments—the defined benefit—from the overall company pension fund.

DB plans still exist, but by the end of the 1990s many companies had scaled back or eliminated their DB plans in favor of "defined contribution" (DC) plans, such as 401(k) and 403(b) plans. The popularity of DC plans changed the nature of retirement planning for millions of Americans. Unlike DB plans, DC plans require workers to set aside a portion of their income and then invest that money on their own. If all goes according to plan, those investments will produce returns that make retirement dreams come true.

Fans of DC plans (including the companies that offer them) are quick to point out the benefits of participating in them: Workers are empowered to manage their retirement savings as they see fit; employers often make "matching contributions" to workers' accounts; investments grow on a tax-deferred basis; the money is "portable" when workers change jobs, etc. But when you get right down to it, companies don't replace DB plans with DC plans to help employees become more financially responsible citizens. They do it to save money. And while it's true that DC plans have several attractive features, it's also a fact that DC plans can make it a lot harder for today's workers to achieve financial security for retirement.

For starters, there is no guarantee that the assets in a DC plan will be able to meet your retirement income needs. Remember, the *benefit* isn't defined ahead of time, your *contribution* is. Here's how it works: Each time you contribute income to a DC plan (via an automatic payroll deduction on payday), the money goes into an investment account that's been established by your employer exclusively for you. While in the account, the money is invested in the specific investment fund(s) you selected while enrolling in the retirement plan.

The value of your investments is not guaranteed, though. For example, if you contribute to a small-cap stock fund through your 401(k) plan, that investment is subject to all of the same risks as if you were investing in a small-cap stock fund outside of the plan. If you contribute $40,000 over the years and invest it well enough to end up with a $300,000 account balance, that's great. But if you contribute $40,000 over the years and make the wrong investment decisions, you could end up with a lot less than $40,000 on your first day of retirement.

If you're like most people these days, a big chunk of your potential retirement income might come from a DC plan, not a DB plan, and from assets in individual retirement accounts (IRAs). To make your DC plan and IRAs effective tools for achieving retirement goals, you've got to understand and feel confident about investing your money.

Company-sponsored retirement benefits and self-guided investing aren't the only things clouding the outlook for retirement in twenty-first century America. Social Security, that perceived pillar of financial stability for retirees, also has been subject to fundamental changes over the years. As a result, almost nobody is promising that the Social Security system as we currently know it will continue to exist in another 20 years or so. It may or may not, and that knowledge puts additional pressure on today's workers to create their own sources of income for retirement spending needs.

One big-picture trend that doesn't bode well for Social Security is the fact that the American population continues to age. As a result, there are now fewer workers funding Social Security payments, but more workers receiving Social Security income. (The taxes you pay into the Social Security system are not set aside for your future benefit, but are paid out right away to current retirees.) Consider this: In 2003, there were approximately 3.3 workers contributing to Social Security for every retiree receiving benefits. But by 2031 that ratio is expected to decline to just 2.1 workers for each Social Security beneficiary.

If the ratio of workers funding the system continues to shrink as anticipated, then the Social Security trust fund for retirees and their survivors will begin spending more than it takes in by 2018 and will run out of money entirely in less than 40 years. Congress still has plenty of time to attempt a remedy, but don't hold your breath for a miracle cure. Now, more than ever, you need to take responsibility for retirement into your own hands.

The Road Ahead?

Retirement in the twenty-first century is likely to be defined by another trend with serious financial implications: the ever-rising medical costs that often accompany older age. Because people are generally living longer than in the past, many can expect to be retired for 20 or 30 years or more. At the same time, however, the burden of paying for advanced medical care is likely to strain the budgets of quite a few seniors living on a fixed income. You can't plan on getting a free ride from Medicare, though—it's facing many of the same problems as Social Security.

As if that's not enough, American women may be at a particular disadvantage when it comes to preparing for retirement. Because women are more likely to earn less than men in similar jobs, because women are more likely to leave the workforce to care for family members, and because many women invest too conservatively, they are also generally more likely to have inadequate retirement savings. So even when it comes to retirement, women might still be forced to work harder than men just to stay even with them.

What Do You Expect from Retirement?

Now for something altogether different. Stop thinking about financial responsibility for a moment, and let your mind run free. It's time to daydream, to think pleasant thoughts about your vision of retirement. If you don't already have something in mind, try to come up with a few ideas now. Have you given any thought yet to when you'll retire, to the plans of other people in your life, to where you'll live or what exactly you'll do with your time? By the way, don't assume that you need to reinvent your lifestyle once you retire. If you want life during retirement to be exactly like life before retirement, then that's your vision of retirement.

When?

The first part of any retirement planning strategy is picking a retirement date. Have you picked the date (or at least the year) when you expect to retire? Many of your other key priorities—such as your retirement account investment strategy and distribution decisions—will likely revolve around that date. So no more daydreaming. It's important to consider how your retirement date will affect other important aspects of your life before you mark that date on the calendar.

For example, would retiring before a certain date prevent you from becoming fully "vested" in (prevent you from taking full ownership of) any company-provided benefits? What about your ability to pay big bills? Would you be able to continue making mortgage payments or tuition payments if you retired before the kids were out of school or the house were paid off? And don't forget the other people in your life, or at least the one you'd like to share retirement with. You can't assume that a retirement date works for your spouse/partner just because it works for you. Consider the fact that for many couples, both partners work and have an employer-sponsored retirement plan, but their circumstances may not be the same.

Let's assume, for instance, that Lester and Danielle are still working, but Lester has significantly more retirement savings than Danielle. If they both maintain their current investment contributions, then Lester would have enough money to retire next year, while Danielle would need to work for five more years. But if Lester kept working and saving for three more years, they could then retire together.

What would you want to do if you were in Lester's (or Danielle's) shoes? How would your spouse/partner feel about your decision? If you haven't thought and talked seriously about the financial and personal implications of your planned retirement date, do it soon. You may discover that you need to adjust your schedule a bit, but that's a far better option than retiring on blind faith and running into money trouble ... or relationship trouble.

Where?

For people who plan to stay right where they've been living all along, the question of where to retire isn't very important. After all, they already have well-informed expectations of what life will be like in the future. For others, though, retirement presents an opportunity to escape the past and to experience life from a different perspective.

Maybe you'd like to use your home as a base of operations and take one international trip each year. Or maybe you only want to travel once in your life, en route to relocating permanently in some new locale. Maybe you haven't really thought about it yet. In any case, you've got to be somewhere when you retire, and the location you choose is going to going to affect your budget in unique ways. That's because the costs of living in one area are likely to differ from the costs of living in another area. Think of it this way: You'd probably pay a lot more money to rent a two-bedroom apartment in New York City than you would in Cheyenne, Wyoming. Other cost differences might be less dramatic, but they can add up pretty quickly. So if you are planning a retirement relocation, you should make it a priority to research prices in that area ahead of time and determine whether it might be necessary to adjust your budget (and maybe even your retirement date) accordingly.

The costs of relocating are only one consideration, though. You also need to be comfortable with the emotional risks of relocating, particularly if you'd be leaving loved ones behind or going someplace you really don't know very well. There are some things you just can't put a price on.

What Will You Do with Your Time?

Retirement rolls around, you end up where you want to be ... and then what? Are you the type of person who wants to spend all day in a rocking chair on the front porch, or would you go crazy with boredom after 20 minutes?

Retirement is a time to stop working, but it can also be a time to start doing other meaningful things. Some retirees take great satisfaction from giving back to their communities by volunteering. Others prefer to stay active by joining clubs, working at part-time jobs, or going back to school. Some live for the joy of babysitting grandchildren, and some start small businesses. You, on the other hand, might want nothing more than to retreat to a cabin in the woods to paint all morning and write your memoirs all afternoon. Regardless of your game plan, the decisions you make about what to do with your time during retirement will have a direct bearing on your spending requirements.

In the final analysis, successful retirement planning requires an investment not only of your money, but also of your mental energy.

How Much Will It Cost?

No matter how you approach retirement, there will eventually be a price tag involved. Above all else, retirement planning requires you first to calculate that financial goal, and then to prepare an investment strategy to help you reach it. While underestimating your spending needs isn't a crime, it can certainly make you miserable later in life. For example, you might be in for a rude awakening if you planned to spend only half or three-quarters of your preretirement income during each year of retirement, but discovered instead that you actually need about 100 percent of your preretirement income in order to maintain your desired lifestyle.

Unfortunately, that's exactly the scenario many Americans could find themselves in. According to the Employee Benefit Research Institute's *2004 Retirement Confidence Survey*, 28 percent of workers said they expect to need only 50 to 70 percent of their preretirement income during each year of retirement. Another 28 percent estimated they would need between 70 and 85 percent. Only 8 percent said they would need 95 to 105 percent. But when current retirees were asked the same question, more than half said they need at least 95 percent of their previous income. And workers who predicted low-income needs for themselves might be surprised to learn that only 22 percent of retirees would feel comfortable with just 50 to 85 percent of previous income.

But as you might imagine, accurately estimating—in detail—the cost of living your life many years in the future isn't an easy task. Unless you're extremely lucky, the best you can probably do is come up with a ballpark estimate based on research and homework. Of course, there's always the possibility that, despite your best efforts, some of your financial guesswork might prove to be way off target, for reasons you couldn't or didn't anticipate. That affordable little lakefront property out in the middle of nowhere that you've fantasized about as a retirement destination for so long may not still be as affordable by the time you're ready to make an offer. The secret might get out about your "middle of nowhere" zip code, and the price tag on your retirement cottage could quadruple before you know it.

Are you overlooking anything important? Are your assumptions about the future rooted in firm ground, or might they be susceptible to the winds of change? For example, have you considered whether you'll end up as part of the so-called Sandwich Generation, called upon to support younger and older family members at a stage in your life when you expected to finally have time and money to yourself? People in the Sandwich Generation might have anticipated an "empty nest," but may end up instead with an adult child in one bedroom and a parent or in-law down the hall in another (or in an expensive care facility).

On a different note ... do you have a secret financial fantasy that you don't talk about much, but actually hope to see come true—such as buying a vintage sports car or supporting a favorite charity? Have you factored that into your budget?

Even if math normally makes your eyes glaze over, do yourself a favor and make at least one sincere effort to calculate a realistic retirement savings goal using one of the many free online retirement cost calculators. Try to calculate the goal more than once if you're so inclined, using different assumptions about the future each time. Every time you fill out the worksheet and punch in the numbers, you'll learn more about the financial challenges that may be in your future.

And here's a suggestion for couples that's sure to keep things interesting: Each of you should do the calculations entirely on your own. Then, when you've both finished, compare notes. Did the two of you come up with the same price tag for the retirement you'll be sharing? If not, why? What are you going to do about it?

Just remember that such calculators are generally designed to provide you with a savings goal, not with an opinion about whether you'll be able to reach that goal. If your savings target seems unrealistically high, you may need to take a fresh look at your plans and start thinking of ways to spend less and save more.

Trend Spotting: EBRI's Retirement Research

Catering to the demands of U.S. retirement savers is big business, considering that Americans currently have about $10 trillion invested in various types of retirement accounts. For that reason, financial industry professionals look forward each year to the publication of the Employee Benefit Research Institute's annual *Retirement Confidence Survey*, which contains all of the latest insights on the nation's retirement savings trends and needs. But you don't need to be an industry insider to benefit from perusing its findings. Taking just a few minutes to study the things other people are doing right (and wrong) might inspire you to do a better job of pursuing your own goals. For example:

➤ About 40 percent of Americans are not currently setting aside any money for retirement.

➤ Only about 40 percent have ever calculated a retirement savings goal, and one-third of them can't even remember the result. However, just trying to calculate a goal seems to prompt some workers to take action: More than 40 percent who tried to come up with a price estimate for retirement decided to revise their retirement planning as a result.

➤ Only 19 percent knew the age at which they will qualify for full Social Security benefits. (FYI: If you were born between 1943 and 1959, you'll need to wait until at least your sixty-sixth birthday. If you were born in 1960 or later, eligibility for full benefits begins at age 67. Retirees can begin collecting benefits before reaching their full eligibility age, but the dollar amount of their monthly payments will be reduced.)

➤ As many as 29 percent of retirement savers said they would be willing to spend less and save more for retirement, but claimed they can't afford to right now. However, when asked if they could save an extra $20 each week ($1,040 annually), 70 percent of workers said yes.

It's Never Too Late, or Early, to Start Saving for Retirement

The nature of retirement today means that we pretty much all share the same predicament. Most of us will probably need to set aside and accumulate quite a bit of money just to take care of ourselves and loved ones in our so-called golden years. Yet we differ from each other in terms of how we'll be able to try to make that happen. One of your neighbors may have a good old-fashioned pension waiting for her, and another may already be a 401(k) millionaire. Another might be a small business owner who's unsure about his retirement savings options. And yet another neighbor, who's never had a job with retirement benefits, might be investing aggressively in a tax-deferred IRA.

The point is, you don't need an employer-sponsored retirement plan in order to save and invest for retirement (although it certainly helps). What you do need is information about which type of financial accounts make sense for your situation, and the discipline and desire to take maximum advantage of those resources, regardless of how old or young you are.

Most "qualified" retirement accounts provide you with two important benefits: tax breaks triggered by your contribution, and tax-deferred investment growth. (A qualified retirement plan or account—such as a 401(k)—is one that qualifies for special tax treatment by the IRS.)

Your contributions to a 401(k) account are deducted from pretax pay. As a result, less income tax will be taken out of your paycheck than if you hadn't made the contribution. Your take-home pay will still be lower, because of your contribution. But because of the tax break you received for making that contribution, the amount of money "missing" from your take-home pay will actually be less than the amount you contributed.

Here's an example: Eddie, who was in the 20 percent federal income tax bracket and didn't contribute to a retirement plan, worked at a job where his pretax pay was $1,000. (For the sake of simplicity, this example assumes no state income taxes and ignores other withholdings you might normally expect to see deducted from a paycheck.) After taxes, Eddie took home exactly $800 every payday. Then he changed jobs.

At Eddie's new job, he still earns $1,000 each payday. But he's also eligible to participate in an employer-sponsored retirement plan, so he contributes 10 percent of his pretax earnings ($100) to his retirement account. Now, on payday, Eddie's taxable income is only $900, thanks to his $100 contribution. And because his taxable income is lower, his income tax withholding is lower too. Instead of paying $200 in taxes (20 percent of $1,000) and having $800 in his wallet, he's paying just $180 (20 percent of $900) in taxes and taking home $720 ($1,000 – $100 – $180). While it's true that Eddie's new situation puts $80 less in his pocket every payday, it also puts $100 more in his retirement account. Not a bad trade-off, is it? Eddie's setting aside $100, but it's only "costing" him $80.

The other big tax advantage of qualified accounts relates to the tax treatment of investment earnings generated by the money you've contributed to the account. Most qualified accounts are "tax deferred," which means that the IRS defers (delays) the collection of taxes on the account until you actually begin to make withdrawals at some point in the future. That can be a huge boost to your investments' growth potential, because investment earnings can "compound" faster—and balances can grow faster—in a tax-deferred account than in an account that is fully taxable every year.

Compounding refers to the process of investment growth that occurs when investment earnings are reinvested into an account and subsequently produce additional earnings. Since taxes don't immediately reduce the value of earnings in a tax-deferred account, the full value of those earnings can be allowed to compound. That's not necessarily the case in a taxable account.

For example, if your $1,000 investment in a tax-deferred account earned an 8 percent rate of return, your balance at the end of the year would be $1,080. If you kept that untaxed $80 in the account and the account continued to earn 8 percent, the original $1,000 would generate $80 again, and the $80 would also generate an additional $6.40. That's compounding. As a result, the account balance would rise from $1,080 at the end of year one to $1,166.40 at the end of year two. If you continued to let all earnings compound along with the original $1,000 investment, and if the account continued to earn 8 percent annual investment returns, you'd end up with $1,259.71 by the end of year three and $1,360.49 after four years. Of your $360.49 gain, only $320 would have been attributable to the original $1,000 investment ($80 per year for four years). The other $40 and change would be attributable to tax-deferred compounding.

There's more to the story, though. You will owe taxes on the money you eventually withdraw from a tax-deferred account. However, the extra boost you can get from all those years of tax-deferred compounding is likely to help you stay a step ahead, even after you've paid the tax man.

To illustrate that point, let's assume that Whitney and Athena are both in the 20 percent federal income tax bracket and both invest the same amount of money for retirement. Whitney contributes $200 each month to a tax-deferred account, and Athena contributes $200 each month to a nonqualified, taxable account. After earning an 8 percent rate of return for 30 years, Whitney would have an account balance of $300,059. By comparison, after earning an 8 percent rate of return for 30 years, Athena would have only $263,662 (because she paid taxes on earnings each year, reducing their compounding power). Even after Whitney pays her taxes, she might still come out ahead, depending on the size of her distributions and her income tax rate.

Time Is on Your Side (or Is It?)

Investing in a qualified retirement account is always a good strategy, and the sooner you start doing it, the better off you may be. After all, tax deferral's biggest ally is time. If you're still young, start investing for retirement ASAP and don't stop. If you're older and you've stopped or never started, now's the time to get moving. If you're already investing for retirement, see if you can set aside a bit more income, even if it's only 1 percent more each year.

Let's turn our attention to the hypothetical Walsh triplets for more insights into the potential relationship between time, retirement investing, and account balances.

Alex, Bob, and Chris all plan to retire soon at age 65. Although they all held identical jobs down at the local factory and earned the same pay, their 401(k) balances will end up being significantly different. Alex will have the most money, having contributed to his account for 30 consecutive years. Bob, who contributed for 10 years, will have the second-largest balance. And Chris will have the lowest account balance—even though he will have contributed to his account for 20 years. That's right, Bob's 10 years of contributions will provide him with more money than Chris, who contributed for twice as long.

How is that possible? It's possible because Bob began contributing when he was young. He made contributions during his first 10 years on the job. Although he then stopped making new contributions, he allowed his entire balance to continue compounding for the next 20 years. Chris, on the other hand, didn't even start contributing until the year Bob stopped, and never could quite catch up. Even though he contributed twice as much, missing out on those first 10 years proved to be a big setback. Table 7–1 shows how the numbers add up, assuming that all three accounts earned 8 percent annual investment returns.

At age 35, Alex began contributing $200 each month to his 401(k). He didn't miss a contribution for 30 years. By age 65 he had contributed $72,000, and his balance had reached $300,059.

Like Alex, Bob also started contributing $200 each month at age 35. But unlike Alex, Bob only contributed for 10 years. He stopped adding new money when he was 45, but left his investment portfolio intact for the next 20 years. By age 65, Bob had contributed $24,000, and his balance was $171,678.

Chris, who didn't get savvy about money until later in life, made his first contribution at 45, and continued to invest $200 each month until age 65. But Chris, who invested $48,000, ended up with a balance of only $118,589.

TABLE 7-1. Retirement Savings for the Walsh Triplets

Alex
> Contributes $200/month, from age 35 to 65
> Total contributions: $72,000
> Account balance at 65: $300,059

Bob
> Contributes $200/month, from age 35 to 45
> Total contributions: $24,000
> Account balance at 65: $171,678

Chris
> Contributes $200/month, from age 45 to 65
> Total contributions: $48,000
> Account balance at 65: $118,589

In other words, Chris invested two-thirds as much money as Alex, but ended up with far less than half as much money. And Chris invested twice as much as Bob, but ended up with about $53,000 less. Why? Because Chris didn't use time as well as either of his brothers.

So far, most of these examples have used tidy assumptions about contributions, such as saying "$100 each month." In reality, however, your contribution is likely to be expressed not as a predetermined dollar amount, but as a predetermined percentage of your pretax income. As your income rises each year, so does your contribution. But you may also be able to increase your contribution without earning a raise. If you're not already contributing as much as you're allowed to your retirement account, then you should think about electing to increase the amount you set aside every payday. You may even be pleasantly surprised to discover how much more money you could accumulate over the years simply by boosting your contribution a little bit.

For example, if you earn $35,000 annually, receive a 3 percent raise each year, and contribute 5 percent of pretax pay, you could have an account balance of $288,618 after 30 years (assuming 8 percent returns). But you could do even better by increasing your contribution gradually, until you reach a higher contribution level. If you increased your contribution by 1 percent of salary each year, until you were eventually contributing 10 percent annually, and then maintained those 10 percent contributions for the duration of the 30-year period, you would have almost $527,557 on hand for retirement.

As with all of these hypothetical examples, there are certain disclaimers you should understand. For one, future investment returns cannot be guaranteed. (And it's highly unlikely that an investment would earn the same return steadily year after year anyway.) For another, withdrawals will be taxed at then-current income tax rates—that is, at whatever your tax rate might be in the future, not what it was when you contributed. And early withdrawals may be subject to a 10 percent penalty tax that is assessed *before* income taxes reduce the value of your withdrawal.

Tax-Advantaged Retirement Accounts: What They Are, Who Can Use Them

Although most types of tax-advantaged accounts share the same general characteristics, there are actually important differences between them that may affect your eligibility to participate or enjoy certain benefits. Not all employer-sponsored plans are created equal, and not all IRAs work the same way.

401(k) and 403(b) Plans

These two types of employer-sponsored retirement plans are each named after the exact section of the IRS tax code that describes and allows them. Only private-sector workers are eligible to participate in 401(k) plans, while 403(b) eligibility is restricted to employees of public sector educational institutions, such as colleges and universities, and charitable nonprofit organizations, including some hospitals. So-called 457 plans, which are similar to 401(k)s and 403(b)s, are available only to government workers.

Annual contribution limits for all of these accounts are the same. The maximum amount that an eligible employee can contribute is

$14,000 in 2005, and $15,000 in 2006. However, 401(k) and 403(b) plans also allow participants who are at least 50 years old to make additional "catch-up contributions" totaling $4,000 in 2005 and $5,000 in 2006. In other words, participants over the age of 50 can contribute $18,000 in 2005 and $20,000 in 2006. Any money you contribute remains your property. If your employer also makes "matching contributions" to your account, you may need to wait a certain amount of time for vesting to occur, allowing you to assume full ownership of the money.

Most of the time participation in such plans is voluntary—you make the decision about when and how to start making contributions. However, some employers try to boost participation rates by automatically enrolling workers through something called a "negative election" feature. Normally, if a worker elects to enroll in a plan, the worker checks a box on a form or fills out some paperwork to let the employer know. But sometimes an employer arranges the plan rules so new workers will be enrolled automatically, unless they check a box or fill out a form saying they don't want to join. Forcing workers to opt out, instead of inviting them to opt in, is how employers implement a negative election option.

But there's a potential problem with negative elections and automatic enrollment, despite all the good intentions. Since workers' contributions must be directed somewhere, employers are required to choose a "default" investment option to receive the contributions of automatically enrolled participants. And in order to expose those contributions to as little risk as possible, employers typically choose very conservative investments as the default option. Unless each worker then adjusts his or her investment strategy to suit a particular set of goals, all future contributions will go to the default fund. But the most conservative investment options are also the least likely to provide the kind of long-term growth necessary to provide sufficient retirement income for many workers. A participant who assumes that an employer has taken care of everything by automatically enrolling him and choosing his investment strategy might actually be in danger of not reaching his retirement savings goal ... unless he takes action too.

Traditional IRAs

As of 2003, more than 36 million American households owned traditional IRAs. What's the appeal? Traditional IRAs may allow you to contribute—and potentially to deduct from your taxes—as much $4,000 in 2005. If you're 50 or older, the annual limit is $4,500. And traditional IRAs are tax deferred, so investments benefit from maximum compounding potential.

Although withdrawals before age 59 1/2 may be subject to a 10 percent early withdrawal penalty, there are exceptions to the rule. For example, the IRS allows penalty-free (but not tax-free) early withdrawals if the distribution is made because of a disability, or if the money is used to pay for a portion of your unreimbursed medical expenses, to buy a home, or to finance a college education. The IRS requires you to begin taking distributions from a traditional IRA no later than the year following the year you reach age 70 1/2.

Roth IRAs

Roth IRAs caused quite a stir when they were legislated into existence back in 1997, particularly among those Americans who earn too much to benefit from the tax deductions offered by traditional IRAs. By 2003 an estimated 16 million households owned Roth IRAs. Named for the late Senator William Roth of Delaware, Roth IRAs do not allow any deductions for contributions. But instead of allowing tax-deferred investment growth, they allow *tax-free* investment growth. You don't get any tax break up front, but you don't owe any taxes on investment earnings when you withdraw the money. It's essentially the opposite of how a traditional IRA works.

Depending on how well your investments perform, the potential tax advantages of a Roth IRA could be spectacular. Not to get too carried away, but if you were to invest $10,000 in a Roth IRA over the course of a few years and then sit back and watch it grow in value to $60,000, you'd be looking at a gain of $50,000 in tax-free income.

Contribution limits for a Roth IRA are the same as those for a traditional IRA. Although you can contribute to more than one IRA simultaneously, the annual contribution limit applies to all IRAs collectively, not to each IRA. For example, you can contribute to as many IRAs as you want, as long as the combined value of those contributions does not exceed $4,000 ($4,500 if you've already turned 50). Roth IRA distributions are tax-free as long as you have owned the account for at least five years and you are either 59 years old, buying a home, or permanently disabled. Roth eligibility is based on income and on your tax-filing status. (Married taxpayers filing separately aren't eligible.) Unlike traditional IRAs, Roth IRAs do not require you to begin taking distributions after age 70.

When lawmakers were dreaming up the Roth IRA, they must have anticipated that some traditional IRA owners would rather have their money in the new tax-free account, because they also authorized people to "convert" traditional IRAs into Roth IRAs. Here's how a Roth conversion works: As long as your adjusted gross income does not exceed $100,000, you can transfer money out of a traditional IRA into a Roth IRA. You'll be required to pay income taxes on the previously tax-deferred money you're converting (the deductible contributions you originally made to the traditional IRA and any investment returns it earned), but after that's taken care of and the money is in the Roth IRA, you won't need to worry about taxes again.

It's tough to make a generalized comment about whether you should consider opening a traditional IRA, opening a Roth IRA, or converting an existing traditional IRA to a Roth IRA. Just keep in mind that the strategy you select should be the one with the potential to provide maximum income during retirement. (A financial advisor can help you do the math as you compare your options.)

SIMPLE Plans and SEPs

With the Savings Incentive Match Plan for Employees ("SIMPLE plan"), an employer can elect to contribute up to $10,000 of an employee's salary ($12,000 for those over age 50) to a tax-deferred SIMPLE IRA. Under those circumstances, employers are also generally required to make matching contributions to the employee's SIMPLE equal to the amount of the employee's salary that was contributed, as long as the match does not exceed 3 percent of the employee's annual compensation. So-called "nonelective" SIMPLEs do not require a contribution of employee salary, but the employer can still opt to make contributions on the employee's behalf. Self-employed workers are also allowed to use SIMPLEs.

Simplified Employee Pensions (SEPs) allow employers to make deductible contributions to SEP-IRAs established for and managed by employees. The maximum amount of the employer's deductible contribution is the lesser of $42,000 or 25 percent of income. SEPs are also available to the self-employed.

Roth 401(k)

Beginning in 2006, retirement plan participants can apply the principles of a Roth IRA to their employer-sponsored retirement savings strategy. Instead of making pretax contributions and benefiting from tax-deferred compounding, participants will be able to make post-tax contributions and then benefit from tax-free compounding and withdrawals. If this option becomes available to you, you'll need to consider which of the two retirement accounts would make the most sense in light of your current and future financial needs, just as you would when deciding between a Roth IRA and a traditional IRA. If lowering your current income taxes now is more of a priority than tax-free income later, a tax-deferred account might be the way to go. But if living without a current tax break seems a small price to pay for tax-free future income, then maybe a Roth is the answer.

Rollover IRAs

These are traditional IRAs that have been established to allow former retirement plan participants to transfer their account balances to another tax-deferred account without incurring any taxes or penalties.

Annuities

Annuities are tax-deferred accounts that promise future income payments based on your nondeductible contributions. If you earn too much to qualify for an IRA deduction, or if you've "maxed out" all of your other retirement savings contributions, an annuity may be a great way to supplement your tax-smart retirement initiatives.

Unlike IRAs, there are no contribution limits on annuities, and your eligibility to contribute is not affected by how much you earn. In general, annuities also offer a good deal of financial flexibility regarding your contribution, investment, and distribution strategies. Annuities usually pay income for a predetermined number of years, or until the death of the annuity owner ("the annuitant").

There are two different types of annuities: fixed and variable. Fixed annuities usually offer a predetermined rate of return and guaranteed income, so they're often the choice of people with more conservative needs. Variable annuities allow you to pursue potentially higher returns by investing your contributions, but as a result they also expose your money to more risk. There are no guaranteed payouts from a variable annuity—if your investments lose value, your payments could shrink. However, variable annuities may offer a so-called death benefit, which means that the annuitant's heirs will receive at least the value of the annuitant's principal investment if the annuitant dies before payments begin. If you are considering an annuity, be sure to learn if it imposes any "surrender charges" on money you withdraw ahead of schedule.

No matter what type of retirement investment accounts you ultimately decide to open, remember to coordinate all of your investments so that your combined portfolio's overall asset allocation and level of diversification are in line with your goals, time frame, and risk tolerance.

Company Stock: Too Much of a Good Thing?

Speaking of diversification and retirement investing, part of the appeal of 401(k) plans is that employers often allow workers to invest in "company stock," which is stock issued by your employer. If someone works at McDonald's and owns McDonald's stock in their 401(k), then that employee owns company stock. If you don't work at McDonald's, you can still own McDonald's stock, but it wouldn't be considered company stock. Sometimes, employers even give company stock to retirement plan participants just for participating in the plan.

But some retirement plan participants end up owning so much company stock that their portfolios are no longer well-diversified. Nothing against the company you work for, but investing a big chunk of your assets in any single security might be a riskier strategy than you can afford.

The aim of this book is not to offer investment advice, but rather, investment insights. Having said that, if a big chunk of your retirement savings is invested in a single, nondiversified investment, such as company stock, you may want to consider rebalancing your portfolio so it becomes potentially less risky. That may seem like heresy to many loyal workers, but just think of all the hardworking people who saw their life savings essentially evaporate when the value of their employer stock evaporated almost overnight. (Remember Enron?)

You Can Take It with You

These days, most Americans change jobs several times during the course of a career. According to the Department of Labor, the average worker holds nine different jobs between the ages of 18 and 34. Fortunately, leaving a job doesn't mean that you have to abandon the retirement assets you've accumulated in the retirement plan sponsored by that employer. In fact, you may have as many as four options:

- Leave the money in the old plan (but retain ownership)

- Transfer the money to a new employer's plan

- Transfer the money to your own Rollover IRA

- "Cash out" the assets by taking a distribution

Some options have no immediate tax implications, and others may result in taxes and maybe a penalty too. Of course, any of the four options will have a direct bearing on your future financial security, so choose carefully.

Leave the Money in a Former Employer's Plan

If your balance in an employer's retirement plan exceeds $5,000, that employer can't force you to take an involuntary distribution after leaving your job. So on the surface, leaving your money in a former employer's plan is the easiest of the four options, because you don't need to take any new action. However, there are potential drawbacks.

The money still belongs to you, of course, but you will no longer be allowed to contribute to the account. Also, the plan may not offer as many features and benefits to former employees as it does to current employees. For example, you may not be entitled to the same level of customer service from company employees, and you may not have as much flexibility to manage your investments.

Then again, if you really like something about a former employer's plan—such as its investment selection—then keeping your money there might be the right decision. Your investments retain their tax-deferred status, and there are no applicable penalties.

Transfer the Money to a New Employer's Plan

If you can't or don't want to leave money in an old plan, you may be able to transfer it—or "roll it over"—to an account in your new employer's retirement plan (depending on the rules of the plan in question). You don't actually process the transaction yourself, though. After you fill out the paperwork requesting and authorizing the movement of your savings, the financial institution that manages your old employer's plan will transfer the money directly to the financial institution that runs the new employer's plan. Tax deferral is maintained, and there are no potential penalties to worry about.

Before you move money from one plan to another, though, make sure you understand the potential implications of doing so. Compare rules regarding any plan features that you may need (such as a loan or hardship withdrawal) to make sure that you'll still be able to carry out the strategies you have in mind.

Transfer the Money to a Rollover IRA

If your new job doesn't offer a plan that accepts transfers from other plans, or if you don't like that employer's plan, then consider transferring your money to a Rollover IRA. Some people prefer Rollover IRAs because there are so many on the market that it may be possible to find one with the exact investment options you want. Also, if an employer-sponsored plan requires you to begin receiving distributions at retirement age, then transferring those assets to a Rollover IRA instead could allow you to delay distributions until later, and thereby prolong its tax deferral until later in life.

There are two ways to transfer money to a Rollover IRA. You can choose a direct transfer between the two financial institutions, or you can choose an indirect rollover, which requires you to receive and then redeposit the money yourself. The check you receive will represent your account balance, minus 20 percent federal income tax withholding. If you don't deposit an amount equal to your pretax balance (that is, the amount of your check *plus* the amount of the withholding) within 60 days, you could be penalized and forced to pay income taxes on the outstanding amount.

Cash Out

Liquidating the investment assets you've set aside for the future in order to put cash in your pocket today might seem like a tempting proposition, but it's also likely to mean that you'll have less money to spend in retirement. Not only that, but cashing out will require you to pay income taxes immediately, and could also cause the IRS to hit you with a 10 percent early withdrawal penalty. And keep in mind that the sudden increase in your taxable income could push you into a higher federal tax bracket for the year of the distribution, so the tax bite on the amount of your withdrawal might be bigger than anticipated. After your tax bills are taken care of, though, you're free to spend the money however you want.

That's nice, but in the big picture, that strategy might be shortsighted. For example, let's assume that Larry is 30 years old and plans to retire at 60. He has $5,000 in his retirement account, but he's quitting his job and has decided to cash out the account. As a result, the IRS imposes a 10 percent early-withdrawal penalty ($500) and taxes the entire $5,000 balance at Larry's 20 percent tax rate ($1,000). Consequently, Larry ends up with only $3,500 of the original $5,000 balance. On the other hand, if Larry opted against cashing out and instead kept the money invested in a tax-deferred account earning 8 percent annual returns for 30 years, his $5,000 balance would have ballooned to $50,313 by his scheduled retirement date. (That makes the $3,500 Larry spent at age 30 seems like peanuts, doesn't it?) What would you rather have— some money now, or potentially a lot more in retirement?

The Pros and Cons of Retirement Plan Loans

Workers who haven't left a job, but who need access to their retirement assets before retirement, may have the option of taking a retirement plan loan. According to the Profit Sharing/401(k) Council of America's *46th Annual Survey of Profit Sharing and 401(k) Plans*, 86 percent of 401(k) plans allow participants to take loans. Within all types of plans that allow loans, an average of 23 percent of participants have borrowed, and the average loan amount was almost $6,700. Clearly, retirement plan loans have the potential to increase your short-term financial options. But as you might expect, there are also potential drawbacks and other considerations that you shouldn't overlook.

When you borrow from your retirement plan, you're actually borrowing your own money and then repaying it back into your account. Plan sponsors can place their own restrictions on participants' borrowing rights, but IRS rules make it generally possible to borrow as much as $50,000 from your workplace retirement account. Your loan can't exceed your account balance, because the money you'll receive comes from the sale of the investments in the account. (Your repayments will then be used to purchase the same types of investments again.) The IRS requires most loans to be repaid within five years, but money used to buy a house may be repaid over longer periods. Keep in mind, though, that your employer establishes your specific repayment schedule, and also determines the interest rate you'll be required to pay.

As a general rule of thumb, you should try not to spend your retirement assets before retirement, even if you do intend to replace them at a later date. Having said that, there are several reasons why retirement plan loans may be attractive. Your loan request won't be rejected, for example, and you won't need to explain the details of your personal financial situation to someone at the bank or credit union. Also, as noted above, the interest you pay goes back into your account; it doesn't line the pockets of some anonymous lender somewhere. And obviously, the money made available from a plan loan can be put to good work if you use it to improve your long-term financial standing.

And if high-interest, nondeductible debt is squeezing your budget to death and you can't get a lower-rate loan to pay it off, then a retirement plan loan might be in order as a last resort.

Proceed with caution, though. Don't lose sight of the fact that pulling your money out of the investment markets might cause you to miss out on future price increases. And unlike interest from a home equity loan, the interest you pay on a retirement plan loan is not tax deductible. You may be required to pay fees to borrow, and you may need to wait at least several weeks until the money is available. And last but certainly not least, leaving your job before your loan is repaid could prove to be costly. Unless you repay the entire outstanding balance within 30 days of leaving, it will be treated as a distribution, which would require you to pay income taxes and possibly the 10 percent early withdrawal penalty.

At Withdrawal: Rules and Payout Options for Retirement Distributions

So far, most of our discussions about accessing your retirement savings have focused on the rules and regulations for getting the money before retirement, even though that's not really the point of contributing to a retirement account. But it's equally important to understand the rules for getting your money during retirement. You know that you can be penalized 10 percent for taking distributions ahead of schedule, but did you also know that retirees can be penalized for not taking distributions on schedule? The IRS wants its share of your as-yet-untaxed retirement savings, and it's not going to wait forever. If you don't take your so-called required minimum distribution (RMD) when the IRS says you should, it could penalize you up to 50 percent of the value of the distribution you should have taken.

Although it used to be notoriously complicated for retirees to determine the amount of their RMDs, you can forget any horror stories you may have heard. Recent revisions to the IRS tax code have greatly simplified the calculation. Now, the only variables you need to account for are your age (which determines your life expectancy) and your account balance. If your beneficiary is a spouse who is more than 10 years younger than you, though, a special calculation will allow you to account for the younger person's life expectancy in order to qualify for smaller RMDs. (The smaller the amount of your RMD, the longer your assets are likely to last.)

IRAs generally require RMDs to begin no later than April 1 of the year after the account owner reaches age 70 1/2. Employer-sponsored plans may also allow RMDs to begin after a participant reaches age 70 1/2, but individual plans have the right to impose earlier RMD requirements on retirees. Plan participants who continue working for an employer beyond age 70 1/2 may be able to defer distributions from that employer's plan until they actually retire, as long as they do not own at least 5 percent of the company.

There are several different ways you may be able to receive RMDs: as income from an annuity, as periodic payments, or as a lump-sum payment.

If your plan allows you to annuitize your account balance (use it to fund a qualified annuity), then you can expect to receive guaranteed income payments on a regular basis, for either a specified period of time or throughout your life and/or your spouse's life. (The shorter the payout period, the bigger the payments will be.) Similarly, periodic payments directly from a plan can allow you to receive your retirement assets over a period of several years. A lump-sum cash payment, on the other hand, puts all of the money in your hands immediately. (Remember: If a lump-sum payment is big enough, it could push you into a higher tax bracket.)

CHAPTER 8

College Planning Syllabus

Is there a college-bound youngster in your life? If so, you probably have another major financial goal to address in addition to your own retirement. Before you start worrying about how much you may need to spend, though, take a moment to reflect on the long-term advantages of having a college degree in today's world.

According to the College Board, the average college graduate is likely to earn at least $1 million more during his or her career than someone who never graduated from college. Of course, owning a college degree isn't necessarily a prerequisite for success (just ask a successful dropout like Bill Gates), but it can certainly open doors and create opportunities throughout life. Unfortunately, college degrees don't come cheap these days, so you'll need to work hard to make those plans for the future come true. (Sounds familiar, doesn't it?)

What's particularly noteworthy is the fact that many parents seem to appreciate the need to save for college, but not nearly as many are actually saving. In 2003 the Investment Company Institute surveyed parents of children younger than 18 regarding their college-savings attitudes and behavior. When asked about top household financial goals, the only priorities parents cited more often than college were retirement and preparing for emergencies. But while more than 80 percent said saving for college was a top financial goal, only about 66 percent were actually saving. On a similar note, almost 66 percent of all savers said they were aware of tax-advantaged college savings accounts (such as Coverdell accounts and 529 plans), but weren't actually using them to accumulate money for college. Instead, the vast majority—more than 90 percent—reported using taxable accounts.

As with retirement planning, what you don't know about college planning could hurt you—not only in terms of the accounts you can use, but also regarding inflation. The average prices for tuition, fees, and room and board have been rising at much higher rates than the nation's overall average inflation rate in recent years. Consequently, your estimates of future college expenses may need to account for the likelihood of additional above-average cost increases in future years, and they should also reflect the type of school the student will be attending—public or private, four years or two years.

The U.S. inflation rate in 2003, as measured by the CPI, was just 1.8 percent, But the average price of tuition and fees for in-state students at public four-year schools shot up 14.1 percent during the 2003-04 school year, according to the College Board. Because costs for room and board didn't increase as dramatically, the average total cost rose "only" 9.8 percent, to $10,636. Private schools didn't jack up prices by as high a percentage, yet they remained far more expensive. The average overall annual cost at four-year private colleges and universities was up 5.7 percent, to a whopping $26,854. (And that's just for two semesters!)

According to the College Board, the average price increase for a year of college at four-year public and private colleges between 1977-78 and 2003-04 was 6.9 percent. Using that figure as an indicator of future price increases, the cost of sending today's newborn off to college in 18 years could surpass $137,000 *per year* at public colleges and universities, and $346,000 at private four-year institutions. Even though almost 60 percent of students get some degree of financial aid, the burden of paying for a college education can still place enormous pressures on a household budget.

At some point, you'll need to calculate your college-savings goal, just as you need to do for retirement. That means you'll need to think about the details of your college outlook: When will it happen, how much you have already saved, whether it will be a public or private college, what kind of outside aid might you receive, etc. Try not to overlook any additional costs that will add to your annual college-spending needs, such as long-distance travel to and from school, perhaps a car for the student to get to work and class, day-to-day expenditures, etc.

After you've identified a dollars-and-cents savings goal, you'll need to put the financial wheels in motion to get you there. And once again, that may require an investment strategy with the potential to boost the value of your savings between now and the time you'll need to start spending. In other words, you'll probably need to make well-informed decisions about what type of college savings account to open and how to invest your contributions. Needless to say, the fundamentals of investing still apply—your investments should complement your time frame, your investment growth needs, and your tolerance for risk.

If your goal seems out of reach, don't panic. It may still be possible to pull it off, even in the event that financial aid doesn't completely bridge the gap. You and the student may need to make peace with a few compromises, but it's probably better than not going to school at all. For example, a student can save money by living at home instead of on campus, or by starting out at a less expensive school and then transferring to the one he or she hopes to graduate from. (If you are considering a transfer, do your homework first to determine how many credits you'll be able to transfer from your old school to the new one.)

Older Americans who want to go back to school later in life may have other options too. Some schools award money-savings credits based on professional or "life-based" experience, and some may allow seniors to audit classes free of charge. (Auditing allows you to attend classes and participate, but usually not to earn credits.)

Paying for College: Special Accounts, Tax Breaks, and More

You may not end up using all of the following tax breaks and tax-advantaged investment accounts as part of your strategy to prepare for college costs, but any one of them has the potential to help you close in quicker on your savings goal.

Section 529 Plans

These come in two varieties: prepaid-tuition plans and college-savings plans. Prepaid-tuition 529 plans are fairly self-explanatory. You can make tuition payments now—at today's prices—for the future college education of a youngster. In other words, assume that a year of tuition at a participating school costs $8,000 in 2005, but your daughter won't actually graduate from high school until 2010. With a 529 prepaid plan, you could pay for her tuition now, at the $8,000 annual rate, and never lose any sleep over future price increases. No matter how much the cost of tuition rises, your daughter's bills will have already been paid.

On the other hand, 529 college savings plans are more like defined contribution plans. You decide how much money to contribute and you choose how to invest your money. With these 529s, you don't lock in future tuition costs at today's price, but all of the investments in the account are tax-free. Earnings compound free of taxation, and when you make qualified withdrawals to pay for education expenses, that money is also tax-free.

Each individual 529 college savings plan is sponsored by a state government and administered by a financial-services company, so no two 529 plans are exactly the same. For example, each plan offers a unique selection of investments, and some states allow residents to claim a tax deduction for contributions to a home-state 529 plan. In general, 529 plans offer the potential for significant investment flexibility as well as high lifetime contribution limits (sometimes exceeding $200,000 per beneficiary). You can make one lump-sum contribution to a 529 plan, or you can make a series of payments. And as the account owner, you're in control of managing the assets; the beneficiary isn't. You can even change beneficiaries without triggering any taxation, as long as the new beneficiary is related to the old one. Usually, there are no age limits for 529 plan beneficiaries.

Coverdell Education Savings Accounts

These accounts, which used to be known as Education IRAs, let you make an annual, nondeductible contribution of up to $2,000 per beneficiary and then invest the money in a tax-free account. Beneficiaries can use the money to pay for qualified expenses at the elementary school, high school, or college level. However, they must use the money for school before reaching the age of 30, or else they risk taxes and penalties on the balance. However, balances can be transferred to another account established for a family member younger than 30.

UGMA and UTMA Accounts

These are custodial accounts opened for minor children under the provisions of the Uniform Gifts to Minors Act and the Uniform Transfers to Minors Act, respectively. Contributions to an UGMA/UTMA account are considered irrevocable gifts to the beneficiary, and the beneficiary assumes total control of the assets on his or her eighteenth or twenty-first birthday, depending on the state in which the account was opened.

One advantage of UGMA/UTMA accounts is that earnings are taxed at the minor's rate, which is often much lower than the donor's rate. However, because the assets in these accounts are considered the property of the beneficiary, they could limit the beneficiary's eligibility for financial aid. Also, the beneficiary is not required to use the money to pay for an education. Legally, he or she can spend the money on anything at all, regardless of what the donor had in mind at the time of the contribution.

It is possible to transfer UGMA/UTMA assets to a 529 plan, but it must be done in a way that protects the ownership rights of the custodial account's beneficiary. In other words, if a parent opens a 529 savings plan for a child, the parent controls the money in the account. But if the parent has also contributed to an UGMA/UTMA established for the same child, the parent cannot transfer the UGMA/UTMA assets to the 529 plan in a manner that would deprive the child of his or her future rights to the UGMA/UTMA money.

Traditional and Roth IRAs

Although designed for retirement savers, these IRAs also allow penalty-free early withdrawals for qualified education expenses. Under the best of circumstances, it wouldn't be necessary to direct money away from one important goal to pursue a competing goal, but in reality there are probably many Americans willing to make such a sacrifice to improve the life of a loved one. Fortunately, the IRS recognizes that fact and won't penalize you for spending your retirement money on someone else's college bills.

Hope and Lifetime Learning Tax Credits

These two tax credits allow tuition payers to lower the amount of their annual tax liability by $1,500 and $2,000 each year, respectively. The Hope Credit (which is subject to income limits) is available for use only in the first and second years of a postsecondary education. The Lifetime Learning Credit, on the other hand, can be used in any year of a postsecondary education, even by students who are not enrolled in a diploma program. You can claim both credits, but not during the same year. Also, you can claim the credits for tuition and fees paid, but not room and board.

Deductions

Deductions of up to $4,000 for college-related expenses will be available for 2005, but not thereafter. Also, income limits for student loan deductions rose in 2001. The full deduction is available for single taxpayers earning less than $65,000 annually and for joint filers earning less than $100,000.

Financial Aid: Seek and Ye Shall Find

Without financial aid, many students-to-be would probably have to prepare for life without a college diploma. Honestly, how many people do you know who could comfortably spend $26,000 on college costs four years in a row? For a lot of students, financial aid is more than just a benefit, it's a necessity.

According to the College Board, there was a record amount of financial aid awarded in America for the 2003-04 academic year— $105 billion, a 15 percent increase from the year before. The average amount of total aid was about $9,100 for full-time students, including about $3,600 in grants, which don't need to be repaid. You'll need to make an initial investment of time as you research how specific financial aid rules and options could affect you, but it will be an investment you won't regret.

While there are many different aid packages available—and many different applications to fill out—it's possible to make several general observations about financial aid. For one thing, students will be expected to spend a greater percentage of their assets on college costs than parents. (Not more money, necessarily, but a bigger slice of whatever they do own.) For another, there are two different formulas—the Institutional Methodology and the Federal Methodology—used almost universally to assess aid applicants. While similar, they also differ in key ways that you need to know about. Unfortunately, neither will give you any breaks for income used to repay consumer debt, such as credit cards and car loans. In other words, you might earmark a certain amount of your income for paying off credit card debt, but financial aid providers won't see it the same way. They may expect you to use some or all of that money for college costs. (One more reason to get out of debt as soon as possible!)

Federal Methodology

The Federal Methodology (FM) system was created by the U.S. Department of Education to determine eligibility for federal financial aid programs, including Pell Grants, Stafford Loans, Stafford/Ford Loans, Supplemental Educational Opportunity Grants, Perkins Loans, and Work Study.

Here's how the FM process works: You fill out the Free Application for Federal Student Aid (FAFSA, available at www.fafsa.ed.gov) and submit it to the Department of Education, which then uses the information you provided to determine what it calls your expected family contribution (EFC). Your EFC, as the name implies, is how much your family will be expected to pay on its own. In general, students are expected to use 50 percent of their income, but the most a parent will be required to use is 47 percent (after allowances for employment expenses and household spending needs). Also, the FM is based on the assumption that 35 percent of student assets can be used for education costs, compared with no more than 5.64 percent of parental assets.

You'll need to have most of your financial paperwork handy when you fill out the FAFSA, because you must provide exact answers to questions about your income (including nontaxable income and benefits), tax deductions and exemptions, investments, businesses, and bank accounts. On the bright side, if your student is going to a public college, then the FAFSA may be the only aid application you're required to fill out.

Institutional Methodology

The Institutional Methodology (IM), designed by the College Board, is a similar system, except it's used by private colleges and universities to help determine how much aid to award applicants. The form you need to fill out for the IM is called the College Scholarship Service PROFILE. As part of the IM process, you indicate which schools you want your PROFILE information sent to, and the College Board forwards it to them, for a fee of $18 per school. The schools you're asking for aid—not the College Board—decide how much you'll qualify for. And because different private schools have their own aid policies and packages, you may not get the same results from each institution.

While the FM does not consider your home equity, the IM does. And where the FM overlooks the value of your retirement assets, the IM may factor them into the equation, depending on each school's rules. Also, unlike the FM, the IM assumes that students will use 25 percent of income, and that parents will use as little as 3 percent but no more than 5 percent of income to pay for college costs.

If it turns out that a particular school's aid offer is lower than you hoped for, and you suspect that a recent onetime surge in income may have skewed your results, you could consider appealing the decision. For example, your financial records might make you look like a higher earner than in fact you are if a recent year's income was inflated by a unique onetime event, such as the taxable conversion of a traditional IRA to a Roth IRA, or receipt of a big windfall, such as a onetime bonus from work. You may also be able to change an aid officer's mind if you've recently lost a job or incurred significant unreimbursed medical costs.

To summarize, you'll need to study up on three areas in order to get a passing grade for college planning: your likely costs, your most tax-efficient account options, and financial aid. That's quite a homework assignment, of course, but it's for a worthy cause.

Although the objective of this particular book is to provide a general overview of several different household financial priorities, anyone with college-bound children should probably build on its lessons by reading more about the college savings strategies they can use to help pursue their goal. If paying tuition is part of your outlook for the future, keep the education momentum going after you finish this book by picking up a copy of *The Standard & Poor's Guide to Saving and Investing for College*, by David J. Braverman. What I attempt to cover in just one chapter, Braverman explores in detail for more than 200 pages.

CHAPTER 9

The Basics of Estate Planning

For many people, estate planning is the most distasteful aspect of personal financial management simply because it forces them to contemplate, in detail, the implications of their death or a loved one's death. With all due respect to emotions, though, it's important not to let them cloud your judgment regarding any aspect of financial management, no matter how deeply you feel about a particular subject.

In the financial sense of the word, your "estate" is everything of value that you own in the world and will leave behind when you die. Estate planning involves making financial and legal arrangements to minimize the tax bills and other hassles caused by death.

Failing to plan for the final management of your estate, for whatever reason, could allow the IRS to grab a much bigger share of your assets than it otherwise would be able to take. That, in turn, could leave less for your heirs. For example, if the overall value of your estate exceeds $1.5 million in 2005, the IRS will impose "estate taxes" after you die, at a rate that could reach 47 percent of the excess amount. If you die without an adequate estate plan, your survivors could be required to spend a significant amount of time and money on legal matters as the courts decide what to do about the situation you've left behind.

Because estate planning laws vary from state to state, and because everyone has unique needs and goals, there is no magic formula or cookie-cutter-type tool for creating a comprehensive estate plan that will suit anyone. At the very least, though, your estate plan should almost always include a legally binding will as its initial focus. Depending on your specific assets and needs, an estate plan might also feature strategies that you employ during life to reduce the taxable value of your estate, in addition to strategies that will take effect after you die to ensure tax-efficient transfers of assets to heirs. In general, estate planning often involves the use of widely available financial tools (such as life insurance and trusts), and may address specific concerns, such as the implications of beneficiary decisions and financial gifts.

Just remember: You don't need to be rich to need an estate plan. Even if the value of your estate is way below the level where the federal estate tax kicks in, you should still think about what would happen if you or a family member were to die tomorrow. Morbid? Perhaps. Essential? Absolutely.

Willpower: Do It the Right Way While You Still Can

If you have minor children, a will provides a mechanism to officially declare who their guardian should be in the event of your death. Without that information in your will, the courts will decide. You might think it's relevant to consider the fact that the kids never really liked Aunt Donna, but the courts might not share that concern. Are you comfortable with the idea of a stranger controlling where your children will live after you die? If not, put your wishes in writing in your will.

When you do create a will, make sure it's in a format that will be recognized by the state in which you live. You can potentially save yourself some money by purchasing a generic "legal will kit" and doing the work yourself, but don't assume it will be valid in your home state simply because you bought it in your home state. Double-check before you spend the money. An estate planning attorney can tell you what needs to be done and can also help you do it.

The process of preparing to write your will involves two steps: taking an inventory of everything you own and need to include in the will, and deciding who will inherit what. The inventory should include tangible property, such as real estate holdings, art, collectibles, cars, items you've inherited, and any other personal belongings. It should also include your financial assets, such as money in bank accounts, investment holdings, etc. If you're uncertain about your ownership of certain property, this is a good reason to dig for an answer.

For example, let's assume that Mike's grandfather told Mike that he bought stocks for him when Mike was just a baby. But if Granddad actually bought them in his own name and only promised them to Mike, then they may still belong to Granddad in the eyes of the law—and Granddad would need to name Mike as the heir of the stocks in his will in order to guarantee that Mike will eventually receive them. On the other hand, if those stocks really do belong to Mike, then Mike would need to account for them in his own will.

Listing your assets may prove easier than deciding how to give them away, considering the emotions that typically accompany the death of a loved one and the subsequent distribution of that person's property. Some of your loved ones might care more about inheriting things with sentimental value, while others may be more concerned about the dollar value. It's up to you to decide how to balance your priorities with theirs. For example, who should get your beloved set of antique frying pans? Do you give the whole set to the family member who shares your interest in antique frying pans, or do you give each family member one of the cherished frying pans? It's your call … if you put it in the will.

While you're at it, is there anything you'd like to leave to a charity, an alma mater, or a childhood friend when you die? Make it official by saying so in your will.

Others Can Decide While You're Still Alive

Another way to address any estate-planning needs that you may be unable to manage later in life is by giving "power of attorney" privileges to a trusted individual. A power-of-attorney designation gives that person the authority to act on your behalf while you're still alive. But don't let the name fool you: The person you have in mind doesn't need to be an attorney.

Lawyer or not, when you give someone power of attorney privileges, he or she generally has the right to access and spend your money without asking you first. So be careful about giving anyone power-of-attorney privileges. Have you ever heard a well-paid athlete or entertainer blame financial problems on the fact that someone else mismanaged the money—and then asked yourself how that could be? One of the ways it happens is by the abuse of power-of-attorney privileges. To put it bluntly, giving power of attorney to an individual who is not financially responsible or trustworthy is a recipe for disaster. If you do give someone power of attorney, always monitor whatever they may be doing in your name or with your money.

Some people also create a so-called "living will," and consider it part of their estate plan. Technically speaking, however, a living will is not a financial document. Instead, it's a document that spells out your instructions about the type of medical care you do (or don't) want to receive in the event that you become unable to communicate your wishes at the time of treatment. For example, if you don't want to be placed on life support indefinitely (or if you want to remain on life support indefinitely), you may need to say so in a living will in order to get the results you want. Again, you should probably speak with a knowledgeable attorney about how the laws in your state may affect your particular plans, and to learn what type of paperwork you must fill out in order to create a legitimate living will. It might also be a good idea to talk to loved ones about what you plan to say in your living will. This probably isn't anyone's idea of a fun conversation, but discussing the issue ahead of time might cause far less emotional upheaval for your loved ones than if they were to learn about your plans during a time of crisis, when it would be too late to have any conversation.

Establishing Trusts and Custodial Accounts

Trusts, on the other hand, are among the most traditional and popular of estate-planning tools, in large part because they allow the tax-efficient and private transfer of asset ownership during life as well as flexibility regarding control of the assets. A trust is a legal and financial arrangement that allows one person to transfer property (to the trust itself) for management by another person on behalf of designated beneficiaries.

When you create and fund a trust, you are called a "grantor." The person who manages the assets in the trust is called the "trustee." Beneficiaries can be third-party individuals, organizations (such as charities and nonprofits), or in some cases even the grantors themselves. There are many different types of trusts available, but in general they can all be effective resources for managing assets while you're alive, maintaining financial privacy, managing taxes, and minimizing postdeath legal red tape. Trusts also owe their popularity to the fact that it's often possible to continue having a say in the management of the assets even after you've contributed them to the trust. A trust can either be revocable or irrevocable, which means that the person who created it either can or cannot dismantle it, respectively.

Trusts are often referred to by their acronyms. Qualified terminal interest property trusts are known as QTIPs (pronounced "cue-tips," like the cotton swab brand name). A common use of QTIPs is to provide for children after a divorce. Charitable remainder trusts (CRTs) and charitable lead trusts (CLTs) can be established specifically to benefit a charity. A qualified personal residence trust (QPRT) can hold title to your home. And a grantor retained annuity trust (GRAT) can let you derive income from the assets you've contributed for a predetermined number of years before ownership of the assets passes to the trust's beneficiaries.

For someone concerned about a spouse's ability to manage personal finances during widowhood, a marital trust might be the answer. In fact, anytime you'd like to make a financial gift to someone with limited monetary skills or responsibility, giving the money to a trust established for the benefit of that individual can be a good way to prevent him or her from doing anything foolish with the assets.

In addition to trusts, custodial accounts—such as the UGMA and UTMA accounts described in Chapter 8—are also popular estate planning options, because they allow you to remove assets from your taxable estate and transfer that wealth to a younger individual. Because you can stipulate that the child does not get full access to the money until adulthood, you may be able to prevent the money from being spent irresponsibly. (Of course, there's no guarantee that the onset of adulthood will coincide with the onset of financial responsibility.)

As with so many other topics discussed in this book, it's a good idea to seek some professional perspective and guidance before you actually commit to a specific strategy. When (or if) you decide that you want a trust, for example, you'll need a lawyer to actually create the type you have in mind. Just remember that the costs of establishing a trust or custodial account can vary quite a bit depending on your exact plans, so try to be reasonably sure ahead of time that the savings generated by the strategy will more than compensate for the costs of establishing and maintaining it.

Naming and Updating Beneficiaries

As you may already know, the word "beneficiary" has its origins in the word "benefit." A beneficiary is someone who benefits from the action of another. If someone helps you change a flat tire, then you're a beneficiary of that person's goodwill. In the financial world, if someone names you the beneficiary of an account or contract—such as a retirement account, insurance policy, or annuity—then you will receive those assets or share them with other beneficiaries when that person dies. (In certain cases, such as with some trusts, death isn't necessary to trigger the benefits; they may simply take effect after a predetermined amount of time.) Beneficiary designations (choices) may even take precedence over the instructions in a will, so it's particularly important to review and possibly revise those decisions when you create or update your will.

For reasons obvious and not so obvious, your beneficiary designations are extremely important. Not only do they record key estate-planning priorities in writing, but your selection of beneficiaries may also have a direct bearing on the ultimate value of the assets you leave behind.

Consider this: By naming your spouse (instead of your children) as the beneficiary of your IRA, you could provide your family with a way of making that tax-deferred money last longer. That's because your spouse has a choice: He or she can opt to be treated as a beneficiary (and take distributions) or to be treated as the account owner (and not necessarily take distributions). By acting as the owner and delaying withdrawals, your spouse would be able to let the assets continue growing. Your children, on the other hand, don't have a choice. They would be required to begin receiving distributions, thereby diminishing the account's value right away. However, while beneficiaries who are children or even grandchildren would need to begin taking distributions, the amount of those distributions would be based on each child's life expectancy—resulting in smaller mandatory withdrawals and the potential for significant tax-deferred accumulation over their lifetimes.

Speaking of spousal beneficiaries and retirement accounts: Employer-sponsored retirement plans may require your spouse to be your primary beneficiary. If you don't want to name your spouse as your primary beneficiary, you might need to present retirement plan administrators with a written statement from your spouse allowing you to name someone else.

When was the last time you checked your beneficiary designations? Has your family experienced any big changes since then that need to be addressed? For example, if any new children or grandchildren have arrived on the scene recently, you might want to list them as beneficiaries. After all, you probably wouldn't want to leave an inheritance to your two nieces and accidentally forget to do the same for their younger brother, right?

By the same token, a change in marital status should prompt you to double-check beneficiary designations. If your ex-spouse is still named as one of your beneficiaries, he or she will still be entitled to those assets. How would your current spouse feel if you forget to update your paperwork and accidentally left assets to stepchildren from a previous marriage instead of to your biological children from your present marriage? The example may seem extreme, but it illustrates an important point.

Finally, keep in mind that if you're named as a beneficiary of a retirement account, you may be able to "disclaim" your beneficiary rights so that other beneficiaries can get more of the assets. This isn't as crazy as it may sound, particularly if you're more concerned with providing financial security for a younger co-beneficiary than for yourself.

Let's assume that Mary dies and leaves an IRA that names her daughter Ellen as the primary beneficiary and Ellen's daughter Amelia as the secondary beneficiary. Normally, Ellen, as the primary beneficiary, would get all of the assets and would be required to start taking distributions based on her age. Secondary beneficiaries usually get assets if the primary beneficiary dies before the account owner dies. But if Ellen disclaims herself as a beneficiary, then all of the assets would go to her daughter Amelia, even though Ellen is still alive. Because Amelia has a longer life expectancy than her mother, she would be required to take smaller distributions. As a result, the IRA assets could last longer under Amelia's ownership than under Ellen's.

The Estate Tax Exclusion

As mentioned earlier, federal estate taxes can run as high as 47 percent in 2005, but the IRS allows you to "exclude" (shelter) the first $1.5 million of your estate's value from that taxation. Between 2006 and 2009, the federal estate tax rate is scheduled to fall to 45 percent, and the estate tax exemption is scheduled to rise to $3.5 million. In 2010 the estate tax is scheduled to be repealed entirely. (It's worth noting, however, that these tax laws and several others enacted along with them in 2001 are scheduled to expire after 2010 unless Congress revises the legislation before then. In other words, it is still unclear whether many current tax laws will still be on the books in 2011.)

The IRS also allows you to give away as much as $11,000 per person to as many people as you'd like each year without affecting your estate tax exclusion. Married couples can make annual gifts of up to $22,000 per couple. So in order to reduce the value of an estate, many people employ annual "gifting" strategies—that is, they give away their money tax-free while alive in order to reduce their postdeath estate tax burden.

In addition to letting you protect your estate from the tax hit that could occur after you die—and therefore allowing you to potentially leave more money to your heirs down the road—gifting strategies also provide obvious, immediate benefits to the recipients of your generosity. For example, your tax-efficient gift could help a child or grandchild afford a down payment on a first home. Or it could provide someone with the financial flexibility to increase tax-deferred retirement account contributions. If those additional retirement account contributions also trigger matching contributions from an employer, then you would be indirectly responsible for helping the recipient of your gift accumulate that extra amount too.

And the IRS allows a special exception to the rule for gifts to Section 529 college savings plans—you can make five-years' worth of gifts in one year. In other words, you could make a tax-free gift of $55,000 to someone else's 529 account in a single year, instead of over the course of five years; married taxpayers can make a single gift of $110,000. There's one catch, though: You won't be allowed to make another financial gift to that individual until five years have passed.

What's Your Situation?

Unless you have more assets than you know what to do with, you probably won't need to rely on every one of the estate-planning strategies outlined in this chapter. However, even if there's only a very limited amount of money and property in your name, it's still in your best interests (or your potential heirs' best interests) to address your estate planning priorities sooner rather than later.

Have you already created a legally binding will? Does it reflect your current financial situation, or might some aspects of it already be outdated? What about the role that life insurance should be playing in your household? Is everyone insured who should be insured? If you have children, and only one of the parents has a paying job, don't make the mistake of thinking that the stay-at-home parent doesn't need insurance simply because he or she is not providing the household's income. If that parent were to pass away, the other might suddenly face the challenge of paying for (and managing) child care and other household responsibilities that weren't a problem before. And what about your beneficiary designations: Are they all up to date? Off the top of your head, can you recall who is listed as the primary and secondary beneficiaries of your retirement accounts, insurance policies, etc.? Look at the estate planning checklist in Table 9-1 to get an idea about what you might need to do.

TABLE 9-1. **Estate Planning Checklist**

Instructions: Circle either "Have," "Need," or "Don't Need" after each item.

➤ An up-to-date will	Have	Need	Don't Need
➤ A living will	Have	Need	Don't Need
➤ Trust(s)	Have	Need	Don't Need
➤ Custodial accounts	Have	Need	Don't Need
➤ Someone with power of attorney	Have	Need	Don't Need
➤ Financial gifting strategies	Have	Need	Don't Need
➤ Life insurance	Have	Need	Don't Need

Also, keep in mind that a comprehensive estate plan doesn't necessarily revolve around only money and taxes. In some cases, the most difficult decisions facing a household are those related to nonfinancial considerations—particularly when the person who passed away hasn't left instructions or has left instructions that run contrary to what his or her survivors want.

For example, the decision to donate organs can potentially save or improve the lives of several other people. But placing that responsibility on others by not addressing it while you're still alive could result in significant anguish or uncertainty for them at a time when they already have plenty of other things to worry about.

Or maybe you think it would be a great idea to donate your body to science. Have you made arrangements to do that, and have you shared the information with the loved ones who might otherwise expect to be in charge of planning your funeral? The same goes for your preference of either cremation of burial, and whether to have a religious or secular service. If you have strong feelings about such issues, take the appropriate steps to arrange things now.

And don't forget that while these decisions aren't what you might consider financial in nature, they could have financial consequences. Donating your body to science, for instance, might not cost anything, while arranging to be buried next to your grandparents in another country could cost tens of thousands of dollars. Nobody ever said planning for the eventual disposition of your estate is a joy, but considering the alternatives, it's almost always your best option.

Before we move on to a less depressing topic, it's important that you also remember to bring together any relevant financial advisors to make sure that all aspects of your estate plan mesh with each other. If you're thinking about making financial gifts while you're still alive, for example, it may be a good idea to discuss those plans with your investment advisor, your tax professional, and your estate planning attorney. Why all three? Because your investment advisor may have insights into which assets you should consider gifting, your tax professional can shed light on the tax implications of that decision, and your attorney can make sure that the trust you have in mind is an appropriate destination for them.

CHAPTER 10

Family and Money

I f there's one thing that just about every family and household has in common, it's the need to manage money wisely. That applies to millionaires just as much as it applies to people who don't have two extra nickels to rub together. Think about it: There are no income limits that affect your ability to get married, have children, get divorced, receive a windfall, or face the prospect of providing long-term care for a sick or disabled family member. The amount of money at your disposal will certainly affect your options for dealing with those scenarios, but it won't change the fact that each one demands a well-thought-out financial strategy.

Money and Marriage: When Wallets (and Portfolios) Meet

Money may not be the most romantic topic of conversation in the months surrounding a marriage, but since money will be essential for the accomplishment of most of a couple's short- and long-term plans, there's really no excuse for not talking about it. With that in mind, it's important for couples to understand the financial goals, strategies, and considerations that can help guide them on a smoother journey through life together.

However, this chapter doesn't address in detail the potential financial implications of your actual ceremony and celebrations. There are two reasons for that.

[132] **The Standard & Poor's Guide to Personal Finance**

First of all, the other topics previously addressed in this book should already have you thinking about making responsible and affordable financial decisions, regardless of why you're spending the money. As almost every chapter has made clear, that usually boils down to identifying your options, doing the homework necessary to determine your likely costs, and then deciding whether your plans are realistic. If they're not, you may need to change some aspect of those plans in order to avoid getting bogged down in more debt than you can realistically manage.

Second, there are almost as many wedding-related financial considerations as there are couples getting married. A beautiful life together can start with inexpensive wedding rings, the cost of a marriage license, and the fees charged by the official who conducts the ceremony. It can also start with a lavish ceremony, an extravagant reception, and a first-class honeymoon halfway around the world. You and your beloved could get hitched alone at City Hall on your lunch break, or you could fly across the country together to kick things off by throwing a party for hundreds of friends and family members at a rented mansion. In other words, the cost of getting married could be quite affordable or run into tens of thousands of dollars. This chapter won't tell you how to plan your wedding. It will, however, provide some financial insights that can make your life together less expensive and more secure than it might otherwise be.

For starters, you and your spouse (or spouse-to-be, who will simply be referred to as your spouse from this point on) should make an effort to understand and appreciate each other's attitudes about money. Notice that I said understand *and* appreciate. Realistically, the two of you may never see eye-to-eye on all things financial, so you first need to be clear about how your outlooks differ, and then make peace with that fact in order to create strategies that work for both of you most of the time.

Some financial professionals suggest that you initiate the discussion by talking about the role money played in your families while you were growing up. That information may (but may not) offer a new perspective on your spouse's money-related emotions and expectations. For example, if one of you grew up in a home where money was usually associated with stress or worries, then that may continue in your relationship as well. Or, history could repeat itself if money was never taken very seriously and having a good time was more important than managing debt. If money was a taboo subject, then even trying to have this conversation might be difficult at first. Also, keep in mind that some families closely associate money with love and affection, while other families never do. Maybe special occasions were always celebrated with cash gifts in your spouse's family, but not in your family. Unless the two of you understand that up front, your spouse (or in-laws) might be painfully underwhelmed by the way you acknowledge a holiday, birthday, or graduation.

Speaking of in-laws, you and your spouse should also talk about the extent to which your money might enter their lives, or vice versa. Will you be expected to lend to or borrow from in-laws, or will that type of relationship always be off limits? What might be the consequences of your decision to take an unpopular stance?

After you've discussed attitudes and expectations, you'll be in a better position to establish your shared financial goals together. In some cultures, it might be normal for money decisions to be based on gender—maybe the husband is expected to prioritize goals and create the budget with little input from his wife. However, this book assumes that husband and wife will participate in the shared responsibilities of household financial management. Therefore, it might be a good idea for each of you to start by privately writing down your top five or 10 financial goals. Then, together, you can look at the two lists to see how much they have in common and to determine which goals are the most important—and which ones can be put off if there's not enough money available to pursue all of them right now. As the previous chapters on budgeting and pursuing other goals have pointed out, you'll need to identify each goal's likely cost and time frame in order to understand the potential challenges you may be facing.

And don't forget that goals that aren't strictly financial in nature can still have major consequences for your financial outlook, such as the decision to have children. According to a report issued by the U.S. Department of Agriculture, "Expenditures on Children by Families, 2003," the average annual cost of raising a child through the first 17 years of life in a two-child, two-parent, middle-income family ranges between $9,510 and $10,560. That's a lot of money, particularly if one parent leaves a paying job in order to care for the kids.

If you and your spouse are planning to have children, have you discussed whether one of you will stop working? If you both want to keep working, have you discussed child care arrangements? Would day care start when the child is three months old or three years old? Have you looked into the potential costs of day care and tried to anticipate how you'll need to budget for it? If you plan to get free child care from family members, you need to make sure well ahead of time that the people you have in mind share your plans.

Of course, the costs of raising children don't necessarily stop at age 17. How do you and your spouse feel about paying for college? Do you both agree that it will be your responsibility, or will you expect your children to shoulder much of the financial burden? If one of you wants to pay for everything and the other doesn't plan to spend a dime, you'll need to reach some sort of mutually agreeable decision and then implement an appropriate strategy long before it's time to fill out college applications.

Other lifestyle goals with big financial consequences include the type of home you want to have and the type of work you want to do. Will your first house be a modest fixer-upper that you'll sell a few years down the road, or will it be the more expensive dream house where you hope to retire eventually? What about work? If one of you plans to change careers or start a business someday, then you should plan for the fact that your household income might decline during the initial transition period.

After you've talked about goals, your next conversations should be about budgeting and bill paying. The basics of budgeting described in Chapter 1 apply to individuals as well as couples, but couples may need to address other considerations too. For example, some people might not feel comfortable in a relationship if a spouse demands to know exactly where every penny has gone. Despite the potentially good intentions of the person asking the questions, the other spouse may feel that his or her independence or privacy is being threatened. Therefore, it might make sense to agree that each of you will be able to spend a certain amount of money each month without having to account for it to the other person. And when you're working out the details of the household budget, you may also want to make allowances for future flexibility, particularly if you're just starting a new life together. Agree to review the budget after the first three, six, and 12 months, and feel free to adjust it if necessary. After the first year, plan to sit down together every six or 12 months to see where things stand.

This may also be an appropriate time to define each of your specific financial responsibilities, such as who will pay the bills every month, who will keep track of overall spending, and how he or she will actually do it. Will you both keep all of your receipts and make sure that the budgeting spouse receives them all in a timely manner, or will you rely on educated guesses from month to month? If you're a guesser and your spouse is a receipt gatherer, you should develop a system that works for both of you in order to avoid misunderstandings and stressful conversations.

The two of you should also discuss the amount of debt and the type of credit histories you each bring into the relationship. If one spouse has a spotless credit record and the other has an ugly history of defaulting on debt, then perhaps the one with the better track record should be in charge of paying the bills. Just be sure to make the suggestion in a positive way to avoid unintentionally insulting or embarrassing your spouse. Marrying someone with bad credit won't directly damage your good credit, but it will be a factor if you apply for a mortgage to buy a house together. Lenders will take your good credit history into consideration, but they'll also base their decision in part on your spouse's bad credit. You might still qualify to borrow, for instance, but not as much as you had hoped, or perhaps at a higher than average interest rate.

Also, how will your financial accounts be managed after the marriage? It's not uncommon for a husband and wife to enter into a relationship with very different personal balance sheets and investment assets. Even if the dollar values of two portfolios are similar, the actual assets each of you owns may have little in common. One spouse might love the risks and rewards of investing in individual stocks, and the other might only sleep well at night knowing that his or her money is invested in conservative, low-risk mutual funds. Will you both compromise and settle on investment strategies that meet somewhere in the middle, or will you each continue to maintain your premarriage strategies?

If the risk lover doesn't want to lose the thrill of "playing the markets," one solution might be to agree that he or she can allocate 10 or 15 percent of a portfolio for high-risk pursuits, while devoting the rest to a more balanced approach. In the event that you have similar portfolios, you should compare them side by side so you can reduce risk by eliminating redundancies. In other words, evaluate the assets as if they were held in one portfolio and then diversify accordingly.

You should also talk about bank accounts. Some couples combine their accumulated savings in one new, jointly owned account, while other couples continue to keep their money separate after tying the knot. Some couples have as many as three accounts—one for each and one for both. Have you and your spouse agreed yet on what will work best in your relationship? If you do decide to have only one checking account, closely coordinate how it's used, to avoid bouncing any checks.

Getting married might also require the two of you to evaluate and coordinate the benefits you receive from work, such as retirement plans and insurance. Again, look to eliminate redundancies. For example, you may not need as much life insurance coverage as you could get from both workplace policies combined. In that case, figuring out which one provides the best coverage-to-cost benefit, and no longer paying premiums for the other one, could be the most prudent option. The same goes for health insurance. The additional cost of adding a spouse to the better health plan could be more than offset by the savings from no longer funding the other one. And needless to say, such a move could really pay off in the event that one of you requires expensive medical care covered by one plan but not the other. Just remember to fill out all of the appropriate paperwork and beneficiary designations to make sure that the new coverage is in place before the spouse who will drop the other coverage actually does so.

And while it would be great if you could both maximize contributions to your tax-deferred employer-sponsored retirement plans, that may not be possible due to other financial priorities. Instead of both of you contributing less than the maximum, it might be smarter to stop contributing to one and to maximize contributions to the other—if one spouse participates in a plan that features an employer's matching contribution and the other participates in a plan without a match. (Obviously, you'd max out the contributions to the matching plan first.)

Finally, newlyweds should resist the urge to splurge when getting settled in their new life. Just because you found the house you've always dreamed of doesn't mean you should spend yourself into debt furnishing it and decorating it as soon as you get the keys. Instead, figure out how much you can afford to budget for home improvements each month and then set realistic goals accordingly, such as agreeing to spruce up one room every three or six months. It might take a bit longer that way, but you won't jeopardize your other financial goals in the process.

The same goes for other priorities, such as buying a car or planning your honeymoon. Sure, it would probably be wonderful to spend a few weeks in an exotic resort somewhere, but if you can't afford it right away, you might need to consider settling for something closer to home. Then, instead of using your income to pay off honeymoon-related credit card bills, you can set aside some money every payday in order to take that big trip on your anniversary instead. That might be hard to do if you start a family right away, but it's a suggestion to help you begin thinking of more affordable alternatives.

As you might imagine, actually having all of these financial conversations may be easier said than done. If you can't do it productively, then you should probably consider bringing in a neutral third party to help mediate. An inability to agree on the dollars-and-sense aspects of your financial priorities might require the assistance of a fee-only financial advisor, whereas working with a marriage counselor may be the best way to remove any emotional roadblocks from your shared financial path.

A Few Words on Prenuptial Agreements

The idea of signing a prenuptial agreement may offend some people, or it may confound others who mistakenly believe that only the ultra-wealthy need a legally binding agreement before marriage to identify what will happen to a couple's possessions if they end up getting divorced.

Prenuptial agreements (also called "antenuptial" or "premarital" agreements) can help ensure that a business owned by one spouse's family remains totally under the control of that family if a marriage fails. They can also be effective tools for making sure that children from a previous marriage remain entitled to receive specific assets or property from a parent who remarries, instead of seeing those assets go to the new spouse in the event of death or divorce. "Prenups" can also assign responsibility for the debts accumulated by one spouse during the marriage and can define the amount of financial support one individual will owe to the other if the marriage ends. In addition, prenups can spell out who will fulfill which financial responsibilities during a marriage, such as paying bills, buying a house, or paying for a spouse's education.

On the other hand, the provisions of a prenuptial agreement can't run contrary to applicable state laws. For example, a prenup may be unenforceable if one spouse tries to use it to avoid child support payments or to deprive the other parent of future custodial rights. And some experts say that prenups shouldn't address nonfinancial matters—such as who will clean the house, whether a wife must use her husband's last name, and whether and how the couple will raise children—because they might cause a judge to question the entire document. In addition, a judge may be able to "set aside" (cancel) a prenup if there is reason to believe that it wasn't signed in good faith—if one spouse failed to disclose all of his or her assets, for instance, or if there is evidence that one spouse was pressured to sign it without proper legal representation. If one spouse had a lawyer but the other didn't—or if both spouses used the same lawyer—then a judge may rule in favor of a spouse who claims that he or she didn't really understand the contract. Also, a judge may view a prenup skeptically if it was thrust on someone at the last minute. In other words, a prenuptial agreement signed six months before a wedding would probably hold up better in court than an identical one drafted and signed the day before a wedding.

All things considered, if you plan to sign a prenuptial agreement, be sure to coordinate it with your overall estate plan in order to reduce the likelihood of future problems. For example, if your prenup says that your children from a previous marriage are to receive family heirlooms that you currently own, make sure that your will says the same thing.

Advocates of prenups say they simply reflect the reality that so many marriages fail these days, and argue that a mutually agreeable contract can allow a divorce to proceed more amicably than if a battle were to erupt over money and property. Opponents of prenups believe they reveal a lack of trust or true commitment. Whatever your opinion may be, don't take the suggestion to sign a prenup lightly. Talk to your future spouse about it, do your homework about applicable state laws, and then, if necessary, get your own lawyer to review any document before you sign it.

Home, Sweet, Home Ownership: Understanding the Terms

You've heard it countless times: Buying your first home—whether it's a condo in the city, a farmhouse out in the country, or a split-level ranch in the 'burbs—represents the ultimate "American Dream," even if you need to take out a six-figure loan to make it a reality. Or, if you already own a home, then maybe the dream is to make it more affordable by refinancing your mortgage at a better interest rate. In either case, whether you're borrowing for the first time or renegotiating a mortgage, getting the best deal possible requires you to think about several details.

Down Payments

In the old days, one rule of thumb was that a prospective home buyer needed a down payment equal to 20 percent of the home's selling price in order to qualify for a loan. That's no longer the case. Today it's possible to get a foot in the door with a down payment in the low single digits.

But while low money down may be the only way for people with limited resources to buy their own place, the strategy can have drawbacks. The most obvious is the fact that the less money you put down, the more you'll need to borrow—and repay every month. Also, a low down payment could cause you to look like a riskier borrower, so you might end up being charged a higher interest rate than someone with a similar credit profile but a bigger down payment. And having less than 20 percent ownership in your home may also mean that you'll have to pay private mortgage insurance in addition to your regular mortgage payments and other borrowing costs.

Fees and Points

Speaking of additional costs, you'll probably need to come up with more than just enough money for the down payment and your first mortgage payment. You should also make allowances for appraisal and inspection fees, credit reporting fees, legal fees, and perhaps a surveyor's fee. Depending on your mortgage, you may also need to pay "points" to your lender or to your broker. One point is synonymous with 1 percent of the home price or mortgage. So if a lender's fee is two points, and you borrow $200,000 to buy a house, then you'll owe the lender $4,000 in fees. ($200,000 x 2 percent = $4,000.)

Not every mortgage charges points, but that doesn't mean you'll automatically save money by avoiding points. In fact, paying points may prove to be a more prudent long-term strategy than not paying points, because a no-points mortgage might charge higher interest rates than a comparable mortgage that requires you to pay points. In other words, paying points up front may allow you to "buy down" your interest rate. Ultimately, you'll need to consider each potential mortgage on a case-by-case basis to figure out how long it would take before your interest savings can compensate for the money you paid in fees. If you plan to sell your home before reaching that break-even point, then it probably doesn't make sense to pay the points in order to get the lower rate.

Fixed Rate versus Adjustable Rate

Your decision to accept a fixed-rate mortgage or an adjustable-rate mortgage might also hinge on similar considerations. Fixed-rated mortgages are loans with an interest rate that will not change, regardless of what happens to rates in the overall economy. One benefit of a fixed-rate mortgage is that it allows you to predict with certainty what your future mortgage costs will be. In contrast, the interest rates on adjustable-rate mortgages can fluctuate after you sign your contract, rising or falling as interest rates elsewhere rise and fall.

You can typically qualify for a lower introductory rate from an adjustable-rate mortgage than you could get on a comparable fixed-rate mortgage, but your borrowing costs could climb in the future if the rate rises. (Your costs could also fall, if interest rates decline.) Therefore, if you know that you'll be selling or refinancing in the relatively near future, then an adjustable-rate mortgage might be a smart move—particularly if interest rates are expected to come down between the time you take out the loan and the time you sell/refinance. On the other hand, if you plan to own the home for a long time, then going with a fixed-rate mortgage might provide you with peace of mind during future bouts of interest rate volatility.

Qualifying Ratios

In addition to assessing your track record of borrowing and repaying money, a lender will probably also take a close look at your so-called "qualifying ratios" to make sure you won't be getting in over your head. Typically, a lender will look at two things: what percentage (ratio) of your monthly income would need to be earmarked for housing costs, and what percentage would need to be earmarked for the repayment of all debts, not just the mortgage. Lenders have flexibility, but one rule of thumb dictates that you shouldn't take a mortgage that requires you to spend more than about 26 percent of gross income on housing costs, or more than about 36 percent of income on all debt combined.

Reverse Mortgages

So-called "reverse mortgages" aren't mortgages at all. They're actually loans for homeowners, usually those homeowners who have completely paid off their mortgages. Here's how a reverse mortgage works: Homeowners borrow a sum of money based on the value of their home, but don't actually sell the home. Instead, they retain ownership for a specific amount of time, usually until they sell the home or die. At that point they (or their estate) must repay the loan plus interest. To someone who is "house rich, cash poor," a reverse mortgage can be a convenient way of transforming home equity into income without giving up the home right away. However, the final amount due has the potential to be much higher than the actual loan amount because of compounding interest charges. As a result, taking a reverse mortgage could help you now, but may mean that there will eventually be less money left in your estate that you can leave to heirs.

"Tell Me About It...": Talking to Kids About Money

With all this talk about marriage, prenups, and home ownership, it may be easy to forget that household financial management involves more than just "adult" priorities, such as finding the right mortgage, paying the bills, and saving for high-priced goals. Equally important is the need to prepare children for a financially satisfying adulthood by teaching them the basics about earning, spending, budgeting, borrowing, saving, investing, and prioritizing.

And since kids may not always come to you with their questions and concerns, it's ultimately your responsibility to open the doors of communication ... and to keep them open. Even if you don't consider yourself as financially savvy as you'd like to be, don't let that stop you—you don't need an advanced degree in economics to give children valuable lessons about money. Remember, you probably still know a lot more about it than they do. Something as simple as telling a story about one of your past financial mistakes could grab their attention and add a human dimension to a conversation that might otherwise strike them as irrelevant or boring. Of course, you don't have to reveal anything too embarrassing. But most people have made "innocent" financial mistakes they don't want their kids to repeat. Maybe you were trying to save up for a car back in college but squandered the money on presents for a sweetheart instead, or blew it on a spring break road trip with your buddies. If you learned from the experience, your kids probably will too, and talking about it won't cost a dime.

In the bigger picture, use some of your time together to help them develop the right attitudes about the role of money in their life. In our society, the message frequently conveyed to impressionable youngsters is that money equals success, power, and happiness. But you know there's more to it than that. You can point out that some of the most influential artists, leaders, politicians, and philosophers began their careers focused not on the money they might eventually earn, but on making themselves better people or their world a better place to live. By the same token, there are plenty of gray-haired millionaires out there who spent their entire adult lives trying to accumulate wealth, only to end up feeling an unexpected sense of emptiness in their later years that no amount of money can fill. Kids figure out pretty early in life that money is important, but they may need your help to understand that balancing it with other priorities is the real key to happiness. So if you see your children being exposed to a one-sided message about money, speak up.

For example, a seven-year-old might think that advertisements exist simply to spread the word about all the cool things he or she can own or experience. At that age, though, your child should also be able to understand your explanation that ads exist for the purpose of convincing people to hand over their precious money to someone else. Most of the time, the people providing the product or service in an advertisement are more concerned with making themselves rich than with making a bunch of seven-year-olds happy. Your child might still want the game he saw on TV, but he'll also be able to view future advertisements with greater perspective.

What's the right age to start talking about money? It probably depends on your child. But don't assume that a three- or four-year-old is too young to grasp some of the basics. When your young daughter reaches the age when she wants to start amassing a pile of coins to call her own, explain how money works. Tell her that money is something that you exchange with other people for things you want or need, and that you (or your spouse) go to work each day in order to earn money for that purpose. Your boss or client needs a job to be done, and pays you to do it. After work, you need groceries for dinner, so you go to the store and exchange your money for the food you'll eat for that night. You can also introduce the concepts of charity and volunteering by pointing out that sometimes people do work not to earn money, but to make their communities better or to assist less fortunate people who need help.

Allowance

There's a good chance that when it's time to talk about money, your youngster will display a deep, personal interest in one subject in particular: allowance. In some families the payment of a weekly allowance is directly related to the child's fulfillment of household responsibilities (such as cleaning the kitchen every night after dinner, moving the lawn on Saturday, etc.). In other households, though, allowance comes with no strings attached.

Those who tie allowance to chores often believe that money should only be rewarded for a job well done, in order to instill a sense of responsibility and to prepare children for the realities of earning an income in the real world. If you don't work, you don't get paid—period. On the other hand, those who don't insist on a connection between work and allowance may not want a child to decide that foregoing an allowance is a small price to pay for goofing off and avoiding an unpleasant task. They also point out that an unpredictable income stream makes it more difficult for children to budget and plan ahead.

Regardless of the approach you take, paying children an allowance can give them an opportunity to learn firsthand about managing money at a relatively early age. Sometimes, of course, lessons will be learned the hard way—for example, if a youngster blows his or her money at the mall food court every weekend, there won't be anything left for that new bike, dress, baseball glove, or whatever. A child in charge of his or her allowance has a chance to develop good habits that will make a big difference later in life, such as identifying costs, setting priorities, and maintaining financial discipline. That child may also learn to appreciate money and personal possessions more than a child who isn't financially accountable to him- or herself.

So how much should you give each week? Some people use the child's age as a benchmark, paying out one or two dollars for each year of their age—such as $10 each week for a 10-year-old. Others parents figure out how much they're already spending on discretionary purchases for the child and give that amount with the stipulation that the child now picks up the tab. There's no "right" answer, though. You'll need to determine an amount based on an assessment of each child's needs and level of responsibility.

But whatever the details of your allowance strategy may be, it's important to uphold your end of the bargain without fail, or else run the risk of sending the wrong message about fulfilling financial responsibilities. If you promise to pay allowance after the lawn is mowed, for instance, then you should always do it after the lawn is mowed, even if you're upset about something else that did (or didn't) happen that week. And remember that providing an allowance is also a great opportunity to begin teaching kids basic budgeting skills, whether or not you insist on having a say in how the money should be spent. On a related note, giving children a small notebook to use as a "financial journal" will help them keep track of spending and savings, store receipts in one location, and generally stay focused on money-related goals and initiatives.

Saving

Will you insist that your children set aside a portion of any income and allowance they earn, or will you merely encourage them to do it? Either choice is probably a better option than ignoring the subject of saving altogether. Point out that saving for goals is something adults need to do throughout life, and suggest a realistic guideline, such as depositing 10 or 15 percent of income into a savings account.

If the child is a bit older and more sophisticated, a low-risk mutual fund might be appropriate.

One way to get children interested in saving is to offer a matching contribution of your own, just as your employer might do for your retirement account contributions. Explaining the concept of a "match" will not only encourage more saving now, but will also better prepare children to understand and take advantage of the workplace benefits they may encounter as young adults.

Spending

As money begins to enter a child's life, your concerns about saving may be in direct conflict with his or her plans for spending. That's normal, but it doesn't need to be a source of constant stress or hard feelings. Instead, use it as a teaching and learning opportunity.

If you're going to impose limits on personal spending, or require your child to begin accepting responsibility for certain types of purchases, discuss your expectations and answer any questions at the outset. Rules or no rules, spend 30 minutes or an hour together so you can reinforce the concept of budgeting and help your child create or update his or her budget. And keep in mind that requiring teenagers to assume responsibility for certain "luxuries"—such as by paying for their own car insurance and gas bills—will prepare them for life after they leave the nest and can no longer rely on you to pay the bills. The budgeting conversation will also be a good opportunity to reinforce the importance of saving receipts—not only to track spending, but also to ensure that defective merchandise can be exchanged or repaired without any hassles.

Another way to create smart savers and budgeters is to involve your kids in the household shopping. You can give your kids the weekly shopping list and then encourage them to clip any relevant coupons from the weekend papers, for instance. If you really want to motivate them and reinforce the benefits of responsible spending, offer to let them keep a share of the savings. Another way to promote financial responsibility is to determine how much you'll be willing to spend on each child's new back-to-school clothes, and then let them choose what they need and want without exceeding the overall limit.

If they make the wrong decisions, their style may suffer but your budget won't. And they probably won't make the same mistake next year.

Debt and Credit

No discussion of money is complete without a warning to teens about the dangers of abusing credit and damaging their credit history. At the same time, though, you should also explain the potential benefits of borrowing, such as being able to pay for college, purchase a car, and buy a house. (In other words, talk about everything covered in Chapter 2.)

Some people even suggest that you go beyond simply talking about credit and actually help your teen apply for and manage a credit card. It's almost guaranteed that he or she will eventually own a credit card anyway, so why not play a role in developing the right habits while you still can? If a credit card offer arrives in the mail addressed to your teen, offer to interpret any language he or she may not understand and explain what all the fine print means. That way, teens can learn about high interest rates and high annual fees without actually being burned by them. But before they actually apply for the card, be sure to announce that you expect to play a role in managing and overseeing the account.

If you cosign for the card, your ongoing involvement should be a nonnegotiable matter. Review statements together to make sure debt is being paid off as fast as it's being accumulated. If a teenager has something to hide on a credit card statement, there's a good chance he or she might not be ready to use credit responsibly ... and it may be time to cancel the card before there's any lasting damage to the teen's credit report and budget. Of course, not all teens should use a credit card. Typically, only those who are at least 17 or 18 and have enough discretionary income to pay their own bills should go this route.

Working Teens

Speaking of income, you'll also need to help your teens find the right balance in their working lives. A part-time job can be a great way for them to start paying their own bills and maybe even start contributing to the household's budget, but it's possible to have too much of a good thing. Grades at school shouldn't suffer as a result of work, especially if college is in the future. And if the allure of a paycheck causes your teen to second-guess college plans, remind him or her that what seems like a lot of money now probably won't seem like a lot of money in a few years. Also, skipping college could actually result in lower lifetime earnings.

Volunteering and Charity

Not all worthwhile work leads to a paycheck. Sometimes it "only" improves the lives of others and fosters a sense of accomplishment and satisfaction that no amount of money can buy. If you're looking for an excuse to spend quality time with your kids, consider working together to support a cause that means a lot to them. It might involve participating in a fund-raising drive, for instance, or supporting a local charity.

What's important is demonstrating that your resources can be a tool for more than just accumulating possessions and personal security. However, you should also explain that there are scammers out there eager to take advantage of others' goodwill. Make sure they know that it's never a good idea to give out a credit card number or other financial information to a stranger on the telephone, no matter how sincere the caller sounds.

Investing

Older teens in particular are probably ready to start learning about the fundamentals of investing, so don't hesitate to chat about it. At the very least, you can explain that stocks represent ownership and bonds represent loans, and that mutual funds own a mix of different stocks and/or bonds in order to help ordinary people manage risk while pursuing important financial goals. Once teens grasp those concepts, they'll be more likely to appreciate the strategies millions of adults use every day to accumulate enough money to finance college and retirement.

If that's a bit too dry to capture your child's attention, try a slightly different approach. For example, let's assume that your son loves Ford pickup trucks. The next time he starts talking about them, say something like, "If you think Ford makes such great products, why don't you buy part of the company?" That will get his attention, and may just inspire him to start checking Ford's stock price from time to time.

Career Planning

Some parents think they're doing their children a favor by trying to steer them toward a high-paying career, whereas others believe each child should follow his or her heart, regardless of the financial consequences. Even if your kids don't choose the path you think is best, there are still things you can do to help improve their future financial lives, such as helping them identify the type (and cost) of the education necessary to enter a particular field. And your real-world perspective can prove to be especially valuable when it prompts them to approach a chosen career from a new direction.

For example, your artistically inclined daughter may have no interest in taking a business class in addition to her art classes. But if you point out that the knowledge she gains in that class could ultimately save her from needing to hire a bookkeeper or manager in the gallery she hopes to own, she might see things differently.

Long-Term Care: Options for Older Loved Ones

Not all family conversations with financial implications will focus on the youngsters in a household, of course. Every year, millions of Americans are confronted with the reality of needing to arrange (and help finance) care for an older family member.

But while kids might warm up to the idea of a money chat, it may be more difficult to talk with a parent or grandparent about one particular lifestyle consideration with big financial consequences: the possible need to arrange in-home care or move into a nursing home or other type of facility. For people who have been independent their entire lives and have never required assistance or monitoring, the very idea of turning to strangers for help could cause hard feelings, feelings of insecurity, and possibly even a sense of diminished self-worth.

In general, though, most types of care require someone to spend money, so it's important for everyone to understand all of the nonfinancial factors in order to avoid paying for unnecessary services. For example, will the senior be able to continue living at home and require only occasional visits by a nurse, or will he or she need to relocate to a facility with 24-hour services?

As you might imagine, arranging for in-home visits can be the least expensive option. But if the need for care increases dramatically, so could the costs involved. Also, continuing to live at home isn't without its own costs, even if the mortgage has been paid off. Expenses such as property taxes, utility bills, and routine maintenance can't be overlooked—particularly if they're rising at a faster rate than the rate at which the senior's own fixed income is rising.

But a nursing home isn't the only other option. So-called "assisted living facilities" may offer the right balance between the need for independence and the need for round-the-clock professional care. Because the amount you'll pay for an assisted living facility depends on such variables as regional costs of living and the amount of assistance required by each resident, it's tough to generalize about how much you might expect to pay. But costs can easily exceed $100 per day. So-called custodial care facilities offer a higher level of care, so you can expect to pay correspondingly higher bills. Residents typically require help with many daily living activities (such as dressing, bathing, etc.), but not necessarily constant medical supervision. If medical attention or rehabilitation is a top priority, skilled nursing facilities and intermediate care facilities might be necessary. In any event, families without adequate private long-term care insurance could face the prospect of paying tens of thousands of dollars annually for care costs.

Once you've identified the right level of care, there are other practical factors to evaluate in addition to price, such as the rules a facility imposes on residents, the quality of food and housekeeping services, and quality-of-life "extras," such as whether the facility offers lectures, classes, or other organized activities for residents. Considering the potential expenses involved, it's important that the services provided will be worth the price. Also, don't wait until the last minute to start shopping around. You'll need time to research the options and costs, and it's not uncommon to encounter waiting lists at desirable facilities.

Expecting a Windfall? Use It Wisely

If you're like most people, you probably fantasize from time to time about receiving a sudden influx of money that would make it possible (or at least easier) to address all of your household's competing financial priorities. But if you're like a lot of people, actually receiving a "windfall" might temporarily cloud your better judgment and tempt you to spend in ways that you really shouldn't.

Although the word "windfall" originally referred to the downed trees and branches peasants were allowed to gather and use as free firewood in medieval Europe, it now refers to any amount of money that suddenly enters your life, such as an inheritance, tax return, prize winnings, or even the distribution you're eligible to receive from a workplace retirement plan after leaving a job.

When or if you ever receive a windfall, resist the urge to spend it impulsively. Instead, figure out how to improve your financial outlook by prioritizing your short- and long-term goals and then allocating the money accordingly. For example, a significant windfall can make it possible to instantly fund an adequate emergency savings account that might otherwise take months or years to accumulate.

If you really don't know what to do with the money right away, consider setting it aside in a low-risk savings or investment account until you've had a chance to think things over and let cooler heads prevail. Just don't make the mistake of placing it in an account that will expose the money to more risk than you want or that will impose a penalty if you withdraw it before a certain amount of time has passed. For help viewing your options from a rational and impartial perspective, it might also be a good idea to ask a fee-only financial advisor for suggestions about the best way to use the money.

Aside from establishing an emergency savings account, one of the most prudent things you can do with a windfall is to pay off as much high-interest, nondeductible debt as possible. Remember, the longer you carry debt, the more expensive that debt becomes. Anytime you have the opportunity to reduce those bills, you should seriously consider doing it. If you're not carrying nondeductible debt, then reducing deductible debt by prepaying your mortgage might be a wise move. Just be sure to check with your mortgage company before making an extra payment to be sure about what strategies are available to you. You might want to know if you can make extra payments whenever you want, or only on the mortgage's anniversary date. Also, don't overlook the fact that paying off your mortgage ahead of schedule could result in the loss of your mortgage interest tax deduction. If that strategy would cause your annual tax bill to rise significantly, you might want to think twice about it.

A windfall might also make it easier to pay for a college education by allowing you to take advantage of some of the strategies explained in Chapter 8. For example, you could contribute up to $2,000 annually per student to a tax-free Coverdell Education Savings Account, you could potentially invest much more in a tax-free Section 529 college savings plan, or you could use the money to pay future tuition at today's rates through a Section 529 prepaid tuition plan. You could also make a tax-free gift of up to $11,000 annually to a custodial account established on behalf of a college-bound minor. (But remember, once that child becomes a legal adult, you can't force him or her to spend custodial-account money on college costs.)

If your windfall comes in the form of a retirement account distribution and you're not yet at the age when required minimum distributions must begin, consider transferring it to a Rollover IRA to maintain the money's tax-deferred status and to continue pursuing your retirement goals. Of course, a windfall from another source could also enhance your retirement outlook by making it possible to afford higher contributions to your workplace retirement account.

When you're thinking of all the possible ways to use your windfall, don't overlook the fact that the IRS might view the money as income and expect you to pay taxes on it. Lottery winnings and noncash prizes, for instance, are generally taxable as income for the year in which they were received. In the eyes of the IRS, the new car a contestant wins on a television game show isn't simply a new car … it's also taxable income. In many cases, the payers of such prizes automatically report them to the IRS, so you won't be able to avoid your legal responsibility by simply "forgetting" about it.

And other types of windfalls, such as those that come in the form of investment assets or property, may require you to look at the bigger picture too. For example, if you inherit individual securities or mutual fund shares, it could cause your overall portfolio's asset allocation to shift, resulting in a risk profile different than what you desire. If that's the case, you may need to set aside your sentimental feelings about the inherited assets and rebalance. Since buying and selling assets would likely trigger capital gains taxes, you might want to work with a tax or investment professional in order to make the most well-informed—and least expensive—decisions possible. On a similar note, receiving property might also require a follow-up strategy. For instance, if the property taxes and/or maintenance costs associated with a particular piece of property exceed the income produced by the property, you might want to sell it. Again, consider speaking with a qualified professional first.

If you're lucky enough to receive a windfall that makes you rich overnight, it could also force you to consider a whole new range of options and considerations. You might want to purchase liability insurance to protect yourself from lawsuits filed by people eager to get their hands on your money, and you may also need to confront the emotional realities of your newfound wealth. Might it cause stress or resentment among family members who didn't share in your good fortune? How will you respond to requests for handouts?

Whether your windfall is big or small, you'll need to make it count.

Strategies for a Split: The Financial Realities of Divorce

At the risk of stating the obvious, most people don't get married with the intention of eventually getting divorced. Yet roughly 50 percent of marriages do end in divorce, and splitting up almost always has financial consequences. Therefore, the end of a marriage requires a well-thought-out money-management strategy to help minimize the short- and long-term costs of going your separate ways.

By definition, a divorce means that some of your plans for the future have changed. In all likelihood, so too will your financial ability to pursue them. One of the first things you should do, even before all the paperwork and agreements have been finalized, is to start thinking about your new plans for the future and identifying any potentially significant changes, such as those affecting retirement, where you'll live, and household income. Next, begin the budgeting process by estimating what your expenses will be going forward. You may not know right away how much money will eventually be at your disposal when all is said and done, but having a realistic budget on hand will add credibility to your claims about your current financial standing and longer-term outlook should those issues arise during the divorce proceedings.

Since this can be an emotionally volatile period in anyone's life, don't rush yourself (or let others rush you) when it's time to sort out financial affairs. Allow time to gather your thoughts, and try to avoid making decisions that seem convenient in the short term but may actually be counterproductive in the long term, such as agreeing to split up assets in your ex's favor simply to avoid an argument.

Also, keep in mind that the manner in which assets and bills are divided will depend in part on state laws regarding the property and debt the two of you accumulated during the marriage. A handful of states have so-called "community property" laws, which generally call for a 50/50 split of debts and property you amassed together during the marriage. Most other states provide for an equitable (as opposed to equal) division of assets and debt. For example, a divorce-court judge may not necessarily draw a line down the middle, but could instead make a decision that he or she considers fair in light of each person's financial standing. In either scenario, though, assets acquired by each person prior to the marriage are likely to remain in that person's possession after the divorce. For that reason, being able to provide records of ownership could help ensure that you'll each get to keep the things you brought into the marriage.

On a related note, you and your ex should be able to keep divorce-related expenses to a minimum by agreeing ahead of time who will get what. After all, the more time your lawyers spend fighting over it in court, the higher your legal bills will be. And considering that divorce lawyers often charge at least $100 per hour (and potentially much more), keeping them out of your lives as long as possible could save you both thousands of dollars. If you can't agree, consider working with a neutral, third-party divorce mediator before calling in the lawyers. Fees can still be high, but at least a mediator will be working for both of you, not against you. Be careful, though, because mediators often don't have the same expertise as lawyers. There's always a chance that one might overlook important financial affairs, such as those with tax or estate planning consequences.

Also, when you're negotiating the division of assets, it's important to look beyond the face value of something in order to fully appreciate what the real pros and cons of ownership might be. Perhaps you'd like to keep the house after the divorce. But would you be able to continue paying the mortgage, property taxes, insurance, and maintenance bills on your own? If not, it might be a better idea to sell the house and concentrate instead on divvying up the proceeds of the sale.

Speaking of selling a house, the timing of your sale could have major financial implications. If you've used it as your primary residence for at least two years during the previous five years, the two of you can generally pocket up to $500,000 of profits generated by the sale without paying federal taxes. (Single homeowners can exempt up to $250,000 in gains.) So if you're thinking about selling and you've only lived there for one year and 11 months, you could achieve significant tax savings by simply waiting another month to sell. This strategy is not divorce-specific; anyone can take advantage of it.

The eventual sale of other appreciated assets you receive in a divorce settlement—such as investments—could also result in capital gains taxes, so be sure to consider not only an asset's current value, but also the potential tax bill you might have to pay after selling it.

Taxes will also come into play if one of you will be making spousal support (alimony) payments to the other after the divorce. The individual making the payments will be able to claim a tax deduction based on the amount, while the other will have to pay income taxes on it. Child support, on the other hand, has no tax consequences for either party. If you plan to rely on the child support or alimony payments promised by your ex, consider making life insurance part of the divorce settlement in order to guarantee that you will continue to receive income if he or she dies.

And just because you're divorced, don't automatically expect the IRS to go easy on you if your ex-spouse was the source of trouble on a tax return you filed jointly in the past. In certain situations, though, "innocent spouse" laws may protect you from paying the price for his or her misdeeds. If you find yourself unexpectedly in hot water with the IRS because of something your ex did without your knowledge or consent, talk to a tax lawyer right away.

Past debts may also remain linked, since you could both still be held responsible for those accumulated by just one of you during the marriage. And if you forget to freeze or cancel joint accounts after the split, his or her ongoing debt problems may continue to negatively affect your credit file too.

Finally, don't overlook assets that have accumulated in your ex's employer-sponsored retirement plans. If you want to receive some or all of that money as part of the divorce agreement, you will need to obtain a qualified domestic relations order (QDRO) from the appropriate authorities (such as a judge). Without a QDRO, retirement plan administrators will not view you as a legitimate "alternate payee" and will not pay you money out of the other person's account.

Of course, not everybody has a spouse or a family to think about. But for those who do, most of the important milestones in life—such as getting married or divorced, buying a home, raising children, and assisting those who need long-term care—carry serious financial consequences that can affect the entire household. That's why it's so important to identify your shared priorities as soon as possible and then implement strategies that give everyone the potential for success.

CHAPTER 11

A Life Less Taxing?

Have you ever heard of Tax Freedom Day? It's the day each year (identified by the Taxpayers Foundation) when the average American has finally earned enough income to pay all of his or her taxes for that year. In 2004, Tax Freedom Day fell on April 11, three days earlier than in 2003. In other words, if the average worker began setting aside every penny of weekly income on January 1 and devoted that money to paying all the different taxes he could expect to encounter in 2004, it would have taken him more than three months to accumulate enough.

In reality, of course, nobody pays taxes like that. But the concept of Tax Freedom Day really drives home the point of just how dramatically taxes can drain money from your wallet.

Although you'll never be able to eliminate taxes from your life entirely, understanding the potential tax consequences of your financial decisions may allow you to pay less each year—or at least to plan more efficiently for the bills you will owe.

Income Taxes

For example, you can't legitimately avoid the responsibility of filing an income tax return every year. However, as the earlier chapter on retirement planning pointed out, you can lower your taxable income by contributing to a tax-deferred retirement savings plan sponsored by your employer. And when it's time to file your return, you may also be able to deduct your contributions to a tax-deferred traditional IRA.

To avoid an unpleasant surprise at tax time, make sure that you're setting aside enough income to pay the IRS what it will expect from you. If you're self-employed, that requires the discipline not to spend all of your pay as you earn it, because you have to pay self-employment taxes. If you receive a salary from an employer, the amount of money that's withheld from your paycheck on a regular basis will be a major factor in determining whether you end up owing money to the IRS or getting a refund.

Your payroll withholdings are determined by the information you provide to your employer on an IRS-issued document called Form W-4. People normally fill out the W-4 when they're first hired, but you can request to change yours at any point after that. Requesting the minimum withholding will result in a bigger weekly paycheck, but may also mean that you need to make an additional tax payment with your annual return. On the other hand, requesting a larger withholding will mean that you see less of your money every payday, but you'll also be less likely to owe the IRS additional funds down the road. A bigger-than-necessary withholding amount may result in a refund equal to the amount you overpaid during the course of the year.

There are a couple of different schools of thought regarding withholding strategies. Some people are more comfortable with a high withholding for the simple reason that it reduces the chance that they'll need to write a big check before the mid-April tax-filing deadline. If they end up overpaying, at least they'll get the extra money back in the form of a refund. But others question the wisdom of giving the IRS a penny more than necessary. They'd rather have the money to spend during the year, or perhaps to deposit in a bank or investment account where it has the potential to produce additional income. If you consistently get a tax refund every year, you might want to consider lowering your withholding. But if you usually end up owing money, then increasing your withholding might be a good move. It's your call.

Another factor that will influence how much you owe is your decision about whether to itemize deductions on your tax return. There are some expenditures that you can "write off" at tax time, such as certain work-related expenses, unreimbursed medical bills, the fees charged by tax professionals, and charitable contributions, to name but a few. However, you're not required to claim each specific deduction you're entitled to claim. Instead, you can claim what is called the standard deduction, which is currently $4,750 for most single taxpayers and $9,500 for most married taxpayers filing jointly.

If the combined value of your itemized deductions exceeds your standard deduction, then filling out the extra paperwork required for itemizing may be a good investment of your time. However, if your standard deduction provides a bigger tax break, then you'll probably want to stick with that strategy, even if you have some deductible expenses. (Just remember that no matter how many deductions you claim, the IRS can use the Alternative Minimum Tax to make sure that you don't avoid paying taxes entirely.)

Property Taxes

In addition to income taxes, local property taxes may also squeeze your budget. If you own a home or other piece of real estate, its assessed value will determine how much you owe each year. Someone planning to sell a house might be pleased to see its assessed value rise, because it may provide the justification to set a higher asking price. But for those who don't plan to sell, a higher home value is usually unwelcome, because it will result in a higher property tax bill. You typically have the right to challenge the assessed value of your home, but you'll need to follow the procedures and adhere to the deadlines established by the local taxing authority.

In fact, it's quite common for municipal tax assessment offices to be flooded with unhappy homeowners each time the local government reassesses home values. People planning to sell often want their homes to have higher assessments, while those who will stay in their homes and continue to pay taxes often try to save money by requesting a lower assessment. Considering the amount of money that may be at stake, assessments can inspire heated emotions among property owners. However, if you plan to challenge your assessment, try to leave emotions out of the discussion and rely on facts instead. For example, researching the prices people have recently paid for similar properties in the same area is a logical way to start putting your current assessment in perspective.

Excise Taxes

You may also need to budget for the excise taxes charged on property such as boats, automobiles, and motor homes. Even if you're driving an old car with a low resale value, you might get an annual tax bill for it. If you don't pay, you may not be able to register or insure the vehicle, and your bill could rise significantly as penalties and interest charges add up.

Money Well Spent: Professional Advice

Regardless of the specific types of tax bills that arrive in your mailbox, proceed with caution and consider working with a tax professional anytime you're thinking about implementing a tax-reduction strategy. Your ideas could have consequences you haven't considered. For example, moving to a state that doesn't impose sales tax or income tax on its residents might initially seem like a great way to eliminate those expenses from your budget, but there could be other trade-offs that negate the savings, such as higher-than-average property taxes. An experienced tax advisor should be able to review your situation and identify the pros and cons of any strategies available to you.

And remember that if you decide to hire a professional to prepare your tax return, you may be able to keep your costs down by doing some of the prep work yourself. Handing over an unorganized box of receipts, for instance, could result in extra charges for the time someone else spends sorting through the paperwork and adding up all of your deductions for you. On the other hand, it might take a few hours for you to do the same work before meeting with the professional, and it won't cost you anything but time.

You should also be aware of the potential drawbacks of trying to save money by preparing a complex tax return on your own. Tax laws and filing requirements can be extremely complicated, and they can change from year to year as new regulations are implemented. Unless you have extensive experience interpreting tax laws and filing returns, proceeding on your own can be an overwhelming experience. Also, any errors could result in costly penalties and time-consuming follow-up work. For those reasons, paying for professional assistance could end up being your lowest-cost, lowest-stress option.

For more information on your tax planning options, you can call the IRS toll-free at 1-800-829-4477 and listen to recorded information on dozens of different topics.

Surviving an IRS Audit

Of course, there's always a chance that the IRS won't be totally satisfied with your tax return and will therefore decide to audit you. An audit is the IRS's way of taking a closer look at the information you submitted in your return as well as any documentation you used to support that information. Since the ultimate goal of an audit is to make sure that you have fulfilled all of your tax reporting and payment obligations, the IRS may compare the information you submitted against information about your income and assets provided by your employer, bank, or other financial institutions. An audit might take the form of a face-to-face meeting, or it could simply be a so-called correspondence audit, in which everything is done through the mail.

It's impossible to know whether you'll be audited in the future, so it's very important to save all of your tax-related records for at least three years. But if you've itemized deductions, the IRS suggests you save related paperwork for seven years. Small business owners and self-employed workers should be particularly careful not to claim personal expenses as business expenses, and not to report workers as independent contractors when the IRS views them as employees. Also, if you are a small business owner, keep in mind that the IRS publishes profession-specific "Audit Technique Guides" to help its auditors zero in on the issues most likely to affect particular types of businesses. Familiarizing yourself with the guide that covers your line of work might help you avoid, or at least survive, an audit.

Regardless of your situation, a few commonsense guidelines can help make the audit process relatively painless. First of all, it's almost always recommended that you hire a tax planner or tax attorney to represent you during an audit so you don't accidentally get yourself into worse trouble by making an innocent mistake, such as revealing more about your situation than necessary. Also, don't sign anything unless you understand exactly what it means and why you're signing it. And if an audit results in a negative ruling against you, you have the right to appeal the results. In the event that you are notified of an upcoming audit, familiarize yourself with IRS Publication #1, "Your Rights as a Taxpayer."

CHAPTER 12

Be Sure
About
Insurance

The stereotypical image of a family in need of life insurance usually includes a couple of cute little kids and two hardworking young parents who each fret about the idea of trying to raise the family without the help and income provided by the other one. Certainly, people in that situation need life insurance, as do other folks from all walks of life.

For example, a highly paid executive with a million-dollar lifestyle might own life insurance so her widowed husband could maintain the family's lavish lifestyle in the event of her death. Or a retiree with a sizable estate might use life insurance to provide money to pay estate taxes after his death, thereby ensuring that none of the assets he leaves behind will need to be sold to raise money for taxes.

And business owners of any age might have uses for life insurance too. If you manage a family-owned business that nobody else in the family is qualified to run, for instance, you could use life insurance to make sure your family will have enough money to hire a competent replacement after your death. Life insurance can also provide money to pay a business owner's estate taxes, so that the business itself won't need to be sold to pay the taxes. If your family doesn't want to continue running the business without you, life insurance proceeds can be used to take care of any outstanding bills the business should pay before closing its doors forever. Life insurance can also be used to pass along something to family members who are not involved with the business. Business partners may also insure each other, so that if one dies the other will have money available to buy the deceased's share of the business from his or her survivors.

In any circumstance, one of the first things you should do is estimate how much life insurance coverage you require. If you're single, childless, not a business owner, and have no plans to leave anything to anyone, then you may indeed be one of those people who really doesn't need any life insurance coverage. Otherwise, you probably do need coverage. The question is, how much? Some people may advise you to adhere to a particular rule of thumb—such as buying a policy that will pay an amount equivalent to five (or seven or 10, etc.) years worth of your current annual income. But that's not necessarily always the right way to go.

Instead of coming up with a somewhat arbitrary figure, make an effort to determine exactly how much money you'd need to leave behind so that your loved ones could maintain their desired lifestyle and still achieve their financial goals. Keep in mind that they might need enough money to pay not only ongoing day-to-day expenses, but also to finance bigger, longer-term goals. Ongoing expenses are likely to include mortgage/rent payments, household bills, grocery bills, car payments, etc. (In other words, everything in your household budget.) Pricier, or longer-term, expenses for your survivors could range from paying for college, to buying a home, to starting a business, or just retiring comfortably. That's a lot to think about, of course, especially if you've never contemplated these things before. However, it's important to address your household's life insurance needs while you still can.

If you're already purchasing life insurance offered by your employer, that's a good start, but you can't assume all of your needs are covered. They may not be. It's still essential to determine your life insurance requirements even if you already have some coverage. For example, assume that Jim has a $100,000 life insurance policy from work. At first glance that may seem like a lot of money. But Jim also has a hefty mortgage, a few credit card debts, and a wife who abandoned her career to raise their three young, college-bound children. In the big picture, Jim's policy from work suddenly doesn't seem like such a fortune, does it? In fact, it might not even be enough to cover his family's needs for more than a few years.

Parents of young children should also make plans for what would happen if both parents died, beyond simply naming potential guardians in a will. For instance, it might make sense to purchase a life insurance policy that would provide income specifically for the expenses a guardian might incur while raising your child. After all, raising someone else's children requires financial as well as personal sacrifice. You don't necessarily need to name the guardian as the beneficiary of the policy, though. You can establish a trust for the benefit of the child, and name the trust as the beneficiary of the life insurance policy. (This is another strategy that you should probably discuss in detail with a financial professional or an estate-planning attorney.)

When you're ready to shop for a life insurance policy, you'll have the choice of two basic types: "term" and "permanent."

Term Life Insurance

Term life insurance, which is typically the less expensive option, allows you to pay fixed premiums (payments) in order to purchase a fixed amount coverage for a predetermined amount of time (the term). If you don't renew the policy at the end of the term, it expires and you are no longer covered. The cost of funding a term life insurance policy can rise significantly as you age, so term may seem like an affordable option when you're young, but could turn out to be quite expensive in later years. One of the key differences between term and permanent life insurance is the fact that term policies don't provide an extra "cash value" component that builds up over time to provide additional benefits.

Permanent Life Insurance

Permanent life insurance is available in several varieties, such as "whole life," "universal life," and "variable life" insurance. In general, permanent life coverage is not limited to a predetermined time period (hence the name permanent), and a portion of your premiums are set aside to build up the cash value saving or investment component. The cash value accumulates tax deferred, and you can often borrow against the cash value at very competitive rates. Some permanent life policies may allow you to invest the cash value yourself in "subaccounts" offered by the policy. Depending on your investment returns, the value of the policy could rise—or fall. The potential for high fees is one possible drawback of permanent life insurance.

The Risk Component

Whatever type of insurance policy you choose, keep in mind that insurance companies view the decision to do business with you as a calculated risk, and they might exercise the right not to sell you the policy you want. If anything about your situation gives insurers reason to believe that you present more of a risk than they are willing to assume, then they might reject your application for a specific policy. In addition to considering your age, insurers may assess your health, your lifestyle, and your medical history to arrive at their conclusion. Insurers may "rate" you and thus make you pay a higher premium amount depending on a number of risk factors.

For example, a diabetic 90-year-old with a bad heart who smokes two packs a day and makes her living as a skydiving instructor might not be able to find an affordable life insurance policy. But being deemed "uninsurable" by one insurance company doesn't necessarily mean you're completely out of luck. You may just need to shop around more and pay higher than average premiums.

Life Insurance Is Just the Beginning

Purchasing enough life insurance is only one part of comprehensive insurance strategy, however. You should also think about your needs regarding the following.

Home Insurance

If you're a homeowner and you haven't read your home insurance policy recently, you really should do it soon. Don't assume that you have a certain type of coverage unless you know for sure that it's specifically mentioned in the policy. Most home insurance policies don't cover flood damage, for instance. Instead, you need to go through the federal government's National Flood Insurance Program to get it. And many policies won't automatically cover damage caused by critters, such as pets, rodents, or insects.

In general, your home insurance policy should provide enough money to completely rebuild your house from the ground up. You should also check to see if your temporary relocation costs would be covered if you need to move out while repairs are under way. Other things to consider include the amount of personal liability coverage and how the policy pays to replace stolen or damaged property. If a policy covers replacement value, then you could expect to get enough to buy a new television, for example. If it only covers cash value, you'll receive however much the insurance company thinks your old, depreciated television was actually worth.

Condo owners should also realize that the insurance policy on the building owned by the condo or co-op association may not be enough. Often, such policies cover only the cost of repairing the building—not the personal belongings each condo owner has in the building.

Car Insurance

Auto insurance is mandatory in many states, but even then the minimum required coverage may not be enough. Bare bones insurance often doesn't cover the cost of repairing certain types of damage. If you pay a bit more for comprehensive insurance, though, you can get glass coverage as well as other types of coverage, such as money to fix damage caused by hitting an animal in the road.

Disability Income Insurance

Disability income insurance, which provides income to people who miss work due to illness or injury, is a fairly common optional workplace benefit and is also available privately. However, disability income insurance may only replace a certain percentage of your salary, and it may not provide coverage for an unlimited amount of time. Always read the fine print to learn exactly how much work you'll need to miss before becoming eligible to receive benefits.

Long-Term Care Insurance

Contrary to what many people believe, Medicare and Medicaid generally won't help most retirees with ongoing long-term care costs. That's because Medicare, which is essentially health insurance for retirees, pays only for a limited amount of medically necessary care, and only after a hospital stay. Medicaid will pay for long-term care, but only after the individual has depleted most of his or her savings. Hence the appeal of long-term care insurance, which, by the way, can also provide for younger individuals who need ongoing care.

Despite its obvious appeal, long-term care insurance does have critics. Some financial professionals believe that the risks of eventually needing long-term care aren't as significant as the insurance industry would like you to believe. They also warn that it's possible for long-term care policies to have so many restrictions and limitations that the actual payout may not come close to providing enough money for the necessary care. Once again, that's why it's so important to read the fine print.

So ... are your insurance needs adequately covered? In other words, what kind of insurance might your household need, and do you have enough? You don't want to find out after it's too late to do anything about it.

CHAPTER 13

Balancing It All Every Day

This book has covered a lot of territory, but all of the chapters have had the same general purpose: to help you better understand the role of money in your life and start improving your short- and long-term financial well-being.

Now, let's put it all together and review each of the key points, looking at them not as separate considerations, but as complementary aspects of the same overall discussion.

The Role of Money in Your Household

Once you've acknowledged the need to learn more about money and to manage it better on an ongoing basis, it's a matter of common sense to begin your mission by getting the entire household involved. The first thing for everyone in the family to do is to arrive at an honest understanding of each one's attitudes about money and financial management.

As you might imagine, maintaining a positive, cooperative outlook will foster a better sense of teamwork than a negative or stressed-out approach. If possible, try to find some common ground and work from there. For example, maybe you view money as a necessary burden, whereas your spouse loves to balance the checkbook and clip coupons, and your teenage children are inclined to see cash simply as a vehicle for pursuing short-term pleasure. Well guess what? You might each have valid opinions. You'll probably never all share the same exact attitudes about money, but you don't need to get too hung up on that. What's important is deciding as a group to harness your energies and make the best of your current situation, for the good of everyone.

Decide who in the house is mature enough to make a meaningful contribution to identifying goals and setting priorities, and then sit down together to do that and to create a budget. Ideally, you'll have enough income to pay all of your current bills and also to set aside money for each of the household's shared goals, but that's not always the case. Since creating a realistic budget involves knowing where your money goes every month, you may need to identify areas where you can cut back on spending. It might require a bit of sacrifice all around, but if everyone starts spending more responsibly, then the money situation could improve pretty quickly. Of course, your shared success requires a sincere effort from everyone. If you claim that you can't afford to save for a particular goal, for example, but you're still spending a couple of hundred dollars a month on unnecessary items, then you're not really being honest with yourself and the other people in the house.

Debt and Credit

These days, the biggest threat to the financial security of many households isn't the need to spend money on the basics—it's the temptation to use credit to buy things that really aren't necessary or affordable. Of course, there are times when borrowing is unavoidable and helpful, such as when you're buying a house. But most often, when people get in trouble with credit it's because they're spending impulsively and with little regard for the consequences.

For example, if you owe so much on a credit card that you can only afford to make the minimum monthly payments, then you're probably in over your head. The less you pay off every month, the more you'll owe in interest expenses, and the longer and more expensive it will be to become debt-free again. Try to transfer high-interest balances to accounts with lower rates, and pay more than the minimum every month. Paying as much as you can and using the cards only for emergencies or short-term expenses are always the best strategies.

And remember: Mismanaging credit won't just put pressures on your household budget while you're trying to pay the bills, but could also result in financial setbacks that continue long after you're out of debt. That's because lenders, potential employers, and even landlords have the right to review your credit history in many circumstances. If they don't like what they see, they can turn down your application for a loan, a job, or a place to live, even if your misdeeds occurred several years earlier. Unfortunately, there's no legitimate way for you to erase bad credit. Only the passage of time will remove accurate blemishes from your credit file, and you may need to wait years for that to happen.

Investing for the Future

If you're like most people, simply getting your budget and debt under control won't automatically make it possible to set aside enough money to achieve all of your goals. Depending on what you hope to accomplish in the future, there's a good chance that you'll also need to invest money with the intention of "growing" its value over time.

There are several ways to do this. One way is by purchasing stock in a company, and in essence assuming partial ownership of that company. The value of your stock investment is likely to increase if the real or perceived value of the company rises over time. Or you can purchase a bond issued by a company or government body, which means that you're lending money to that organization. At the most basic level, bond investors make money by collecting the interest payments provided by the lender between the time the bond is issued and the time the loan is repaid. But bond investments can also be bought and sold in the meantime, and bond investors can make (or lose) money based on whether their bonds are selling on the "secondary market" for more (or less) than their original price.

The potential returns that may be provided by a particular investment are usually inversely proportional to the risks involved with owning that investment. In general, the riskiest investments are those with prices that fluctuate the most in the short term. However, riskier investments typically also have the potential to provide higher long-term returns than "safer" investments. Stock prices are typically much more volatile on a short-term basis than bond prices, for instance, but throughout history stocks have also tended to produce the most impressive average long-term gains. So-called money market investments, which represent very short-term debts, have traditionally provided the least amount of price volatility, but also the lowest average annual returns.

The key to managing risk in your investment portfolio is the use of a strategy called "diversification," which has been described as the opposite of putting all your eggs in one basket. By spreading your money among a diversified mix of different investments, you may be able to protect the overall value of your portfolio from being adversely affected by a decline in the value of any one investment. For many individuals, the best way to achieve an adequate level of diversification is to invest in mutual funds. That's because each mutual fund employs financial professionals to purchase many different stocks, bonds, and/or money market investments on behalf of the fund's shareholders. When the overall value of these combined holdings rises or falls, so does the value of a mutual fund investment.

Regardless of whether you purchase individual stocks and bonds or mutual fund shares, your particular asset allocation (investment mix) should reflect three things: your financial goal, your time frame, and your personal tolerance for risk. If you're investing for a long-term goal, it's generally a good idea to stay focused on that goal regardless of the market's short-term ups and downs. However, you should make a point of reviewing your investment strategy once or twice a year to confirm that it's still appropriate for your needs.

Retirement

Retirement is a perfect example of a long-term financial goal that will almost certainly require you to implement an investment strategy. First of all, the Social Security system is facing an uncertain future, due to the fact that as time goes on, fewer workers are paying for current benefits while more retirees are collecting benefits. Also, many companies no longer offer guaranteed pensions. Instead, they offer "defined contribution" retirement plans that require workers to set aside and manage their own money for retirement in tax-deferred investment accounts.

If your employer offers a defined contribution plan, such as a 401(k) plan, you may want to sign up and start setting aside as much income as you can afford. If you're lucky, your employer may also make a "matching contribution" to your account every time you contribute some of your own money. Your contributions reduce your take-home pay but also have two favorable results: less taxes are withheld from your paycheck, and the money you contribute remains your property. Your take-home pay is reduced by an amount less than what you contribute—because the contribution lowers the amount of your taxable income. When you eventually withdraw the money in retirement, you'll owe taxes at then-current income tax rates. (If you withdraw the money before retirement, you may also have to pay a 10 percent penalty.)

Individual retirement accounts (IRAs), which are tax-advantaged accounts you set up on your own, may also make sense for your retirement savings strategy—particularly if you want to move money out of a former employer's retirement savings plan without incurring penalties or immediate taxation.

In general, most retirement accounts will eventually require you to start taking mandatory withdrawals—called required minimum distributions—after you reach age 70 1/2.

College Planning

The other big goal that often calls for an investment strategy is paying for a college education. And just as there are special accounts designed to help people save for retirement while minimizing the taxes that would normally be associated with investing, there are also several tax-efficient ways to prepare for college costs.

Section 529 college savings plans and Coverdell Education Savings Accounts allow your investment earnings to grow tax-free. You can also withdraw the money tax-free, as long as you spend it on qualified education expenses. And Section 529 prepaid tuition plans allow you to pay for a future education at current prices. Contributing money to a custodial account for a minor may also be an effective way for you to help pave the way for college. However, your son or daughter (or grandson or granddaughter) won't necessarily have to spend the money on college after gaining access to it as a young adult. Although the average annual cost of attending a private, four-year college now exceeds $26,000, many students actually pay less than that, thanks to financial aid packages. Needless to say, the key to getting as much aid as possible is to fill out the proper applications and submit them on time.

Estate Planning

It's a fact of life that no plan for the future is complete until it accounts for what will happen after your death or the death of others in your family. That's what your estate plan is for. Writing a legally binding will that outlines where all of your possessions will go after you die is the foundation of an estate plan, but a will alone may not be enough to address all of your needs. It's important, for instance, to have enough life insurance coverage so that payments will allow your survivors to maintain their quality of life and continue to pursue big financial goals, such as paying for college and retiring with confidence.

If the value of your possessions exceeds $1.5 million (2005 limit) at the time of your death, the federal government will impose estate taxes at rates that can go as high as 47 percent (2005 limit) on the excess amount. Therefore, people who have amassed a significant amount of assets often employ gift-giving strategies to reduce the value of their estate before death. For example, the IRS allows you to give away as much as $11,000 annually to an unlimited number of people without triggering any taxation. Of course, many people aren't in a position to give away money like that, but there are other estate planning strategies that nobody should overlook, such as confirming that the beneficiary designations on your financial accounts and life insurance policies are all up to date.

Family and Money

If your plans for the future include getting married, getting divorced, buying a house, teaching children about money, or helping to provide care for older loved ones, then you and your family members should work together to understand and minimize the likely costs involved. Thus, when two people decide to get married, they need to communicate openly and honestly about their shared financial goals, as well as the attitudes and expectations each one has about money. It may not be realistic to expect your partner to share all of your priorities, but if you each know where the other stands on important issues, it can help you stay focused on goals and manage the stress that sometimes arises from financial disagreements. Although stress may be hard to avoid during a divorce, there are ways to keep costs down. If the two of you can reach an amicable agreement about how to split household assets, then you won't need to pay lawyers to take care of that job for you.

Another potentially difficult and expensive situation that you may need to address within the family is how to provide care for an older relative who is no longer able to live completely independently. Since costs typically rise as more care is required, you shouldn't be spending, or overspending, for services or facilities that aren't strictly necessary. Your input can also make a big difference in a child's future quality of life. By taking the time to teach a youngster about basic financial management skills and considerations, you'll prepare him or her for a more financially secure adulthood. And you can do everyone in the house a favor by resisting the urge to spend a windfall impulsively. Put the money to good use by paying off debt, creating an emergency savings account, setting aside money for college or retirement, etc.

Taxes

You can't escape from taxes, but you can take steps to minimize their influence on your budget. For example, you should always consider taking advantage of tax-efficient retirement savings accounts. And adjusting your payroll tax withholdings could spare you from the unpleasant surprise of discovering that you owe additional taxes when you file your return. Because paying taxes and dealing with the IRS can be extraordinarily complex, you should probably consult a tax professional whenever you review your strategy or face an IRS audit.

Insurance

No matter how well you budget, save, invest, and plan, purchasing enough insurance coverage for all of your household's needs may be the only way to protect your financial security from an unexpected setback. Do you have adequate homeowner's (or renter's) insurance, auto insurance, life insurance, long-term care insurance, disability insurance, and, if necessary, business liability insurance? If not, just one or two unfortunate situations could require you to spend money that had been earmarked for other purposes, putting your entire set of short- and long-term goals in jeopardy.

Getting Ready for an Annual Review

None of the financial priorities discussed in this book exists in a vacuum. You should view them all as indispensable and complementary components of a comprehensive financial plan that will help you move through life with focus and confidence.

To prevent your plan from becoming obsolete, you and your family members need to review your entire range of priorities and strategies once every six or 12 months. In Table 13–1, on the next page, you'll see a comprehensive financial planning list, and in Table 13–2, a worksheet to help you review your financial situation. If you're not comfortable doing it without professional assistance, budget some money to hire a fee-only financial advisor who can lend a hand.

Someday, you'll look back on your decision to get serious about money with a sense of pride, satisfaction, and accomplishment. Since this is the end of the book, allow me to say "Congratulations!" now.

TABLE 13-1. Overall Financial Planning Checklist

➤ Have you created a comprehensive budget?	Yes	No
➤ Do you have enough emergency savings?	Yes	No
➤ Have you recently reviewed your credit history for accuracy?	Yes	No
➤ Are you aggressively paying off debt?	Yes	No
➤ Have you consolidated high-interest debt?	Yes	No
➤ Have you identified your investment goals and risk tolerance?	Yes	No
➤ Does your asset allocation reflect those investment needs?	Yes	No
➤ If not, have you made plans to rebalance?	Yes	No
➤ Do you know which benchmarks/indexes best reflect your investments?	Yes	No
➤ Are you contributing as much as possible to retirement accounts?	Yes	No
➤ Have you calculated a retirement savings goal?	Yes	No
➤ Are you doing everything possible to prepare for college costs?	Yes	No
➤ Do you have a comprehensive, up-to-date estate plan?	Yes	No
➤ Are you teaching your children to use money responsibly?	Yes	No
➤ Are you taking steps to prepare for a loved one's long-term care needs?	Yes	No
➤ Have you determined if itemizing tax deductions would save money?	Yes	No
➤ Do you own adequate life insurance and disability insurance?	Yes	No
➤ Do you meet with a financial advisor at least once each year?	Yes	No

Table 13-2. Worksheet for Financial Review(s)

Date of current review _____

Action taken since last review_____

_____

_____

_____

Top priorities of current review _____

_____

_____

_____

New priorities identified during current review _____

_____

_____

_____

Action to be taken as result of review _____

_____

_____

_____

Date of next review_____

Priorities for next review _____

_____

_____

_____

General notes regarding current review and future plans_____

_____

_____

_____

Index

Index

Emergency savings account
  financial crisis requiring, 9
  requiring self discipline for, 11
  selecting proper account for, 11
Employee Benefit Research Institute
  (EBRI), 91
Employer-sponsored retirement plan,
  104
  divorce including, 156
  tax deferred benefit of, 93
Equal Credit Opportunity Act (ECOA),
  28
Equities. *See* Stocks
Equity income fund, 60
Estate planning
  checklist for, 128
  estate taxes in, 174
  financial advisors in, 129
  financial/legal arrangements for,
    119–120
  gifting strategies used in, 174
  judgment clouded for, 119
  legally binding will for, 174
  life insurance role in, 127, 174
  organ donation in, 128–129
  trusts as, 122–123
  will as part of, 120
Estate tax exclusion, 126
Estate taxes
  estate planning with, 174
  gifting strategies and, 126
  IRS possibly imposing, 119
Exchange-traded funds (ETFs), 79
Excise tax, 160
Expected family contributions (EFC),
  115

Face value, 47
Fair Credit Billing Act (FCBA), 28–29
Fair Credit Reporting Act (FCRA)
  Federal Trade Commission
    enforcing, 27
  rights protected under, 27–28
Fair Debt Collections Act (FDCA)
  consumers protected with, 29
  right established by, 29

Fannie Mae, 50
FCBA. *See* Fair Credit Billing Act
FCRA. *See* Fair Credit Reporting Act
Federal estate taxes, 126
Federal financial aid programs, 115
Federal government bonds, 49
Federal Methodology (FM), 115–116
Federal National Mortgage
  Association, 50
Federal Reserve, 53
Federal Trade Commission (FTC)
  FCRA enforced by, 27
  web site, letter format from, 32
Financial advisors, 129
Financial aid, 110
  finding, 114–117
  methodologies for determining, 115
  record amount of, 114–115
Financial assets, 121
Financial confidence, 1
Financial goals, 172–173
  achieving, 8
  confidence accomplishing, 1
  couples understanding, 131
  discussing, 5
  identifying, 5
  investments having, 70
  objectives for, 5–6
  retirement with, 90
Financial planning
  checklist for, 177
  debt counseling agencies assisting,
    34
  divorce requiring, 175
  evaluating situation for, 6
  financial questions by, 81
  preparing to work with, 80–81
  rate of inflation for, 71
  requiring self discipline for, 11
  wedding related expenses for, 132
Financial reviews (worksheet), 178
Financial security
  debt threatening, 13
  groundwork for, 2
  responsibilities for, 4
529 plans, 112–113, 127, 152, 173–174

About the Author

Tom Downey is a financial writer for Standard & Poor's Financial Communications.

FREE OFFER—The Oldest and Wisest Investment Newsletter in the Newest and Easiest Format

The Outlook is America's oldest continuously published investment advisory newsletter, and now it's available online! Best of all, because you're reading an S&P book, you're entitled to a free 30-day trial. Outlook Online is perfect for both beginners and expert investors alike. The site contains the latest issue of *The Outlook* as well as a searchable archive of the past year's issues. You'll get everything from Standard & Poor's latest individual investment recommendations and economic forecasts to complete portfolios that can help you build wealth. For more than 80 years, *The Outlook* has been identifying the developments that affect stock performance—and making recommendations on when to buy, sell and hold. With Outlook Online you'll also get:

Features on Sectors, Industries and Technical Analysis—These weekly articles will keep you informed about what sectors are poised to outperform, what industries have been on a roll, a where the market may be headed next.

Supervised Master List of Recommended Issues—Standard & Poor's favorites for long-term capital appreciation and superior long-term total return. These groups of stocks have been helping generations of investors build wealth.

Complete Lists of STARS stocks—The highly regarded *Stock Appreciation Ranking System* offers an easy way to pick stocks that Standard & Poor's believes will do best in the near term—six months to one year. Week after week, STARS ranks 1,200 active stocks so you can track changes at a glance.

Platinum and Neural Fair Value Portfolios—Outlook Online also contains detailed information on two more of Standard & Poor's portfolios, both of which have historically outperformed the market by wide margins.

Global Features—Outlook Online is also helpful to investors looking for news and views from abroad. It contains a number of features on both Europe and Asia, including the best picks from S&P's overseas research departments.

Stock and Fund Reports—You'll even get access to 10 free Standard & Poor's reports every month. Whether you're looking for more information on a company or a mutual fund, these reports will help you make informed decisions.

It's simple to activate your free trial to Outlook Online. Just visit the URL below and follow the directions on the screen. No credit card is required and registration will take only a few minutes. To get the best guidance on Wall Street and specific stock recommendations from the experts in the field, just visit us at:

http://www.spoutlookonline.com/ol_mw1.0.asp?ADID=DOW